T0330446

Mathematical Principles of Economics

CLASSICS IN THE HISTORY OF ECONOMICS

General Editor: Mark Blaug, *Professor Emeritus, University of London; Consultant Professor, University of Buckingham; and Visiting Professor, University of Exeter*

This important new series comprises reprints of classic books in economics with new introductions by leading contemporary economists. Under the direction of Mark Blaug – who is recognized to be a leading world authority on the history of economic thought – the series will comprise classic works which have hitherto been unavailable.

The Co-ordination of the Laws of Distribution
Philip H. Wicksteed
Revised edition with an introduction by Ian Steedman

Mathematical Principles of Economics
Carl Friedrich Wilhelm Launhardt
English translation edited with an introduction by John Creedy

Mathematical Principles of Economics

Wilhelm Launhardt

Translated by Hilda Schmidt
Edited and with an introduction by John Creedy
The Truby Williams Professor of Economics,
The University of Melbourne

Classics in the History of Economics

Edward Elgar

Published by
Edward Elgar Publishing Limited
Gower House
Croft Road
Aldershot
Hants GU11 3HR
England

Edward Elgar Publishing Company
Old Post Road
Brookfield
Vermont 05036
USA

A CIP catalogue record for this book is available from the British Library

A CIP catalogue record for this book is available from the US Library of Congress

ISBN 1 85278 723 6

Contents

Contents

Acknowledgements

The initial translation of Launhardt's *Mathematical Principles of Economics* was financed by a small grant from the Research Fund of the University of Melbourne Faculty of Economics and Commerce, for which I am very grateful. The burden of word processing the numerous iterations was borne cheerfully by Julie Carter, Margaret Lochran, Sally Nolan and Lynne Ki, to whom I am very grateful. The invaluable encouragement of Professor Denis O'Brien is, as ever, greatly appreciated.

Introduction
John Creedy

Carl Friedrich Wilhelm Launhardt was born in Hanover, Germany, on 4 April 1832. The whole of his professional life was spent in Hanover, where he died on 14 May 1918. From 1869 Launhardt was Professor of Roads, Railways and Bridges at the Hanover Polytechnic Institute, and later served as its Director. When the Institute became the Technische Hochschule, Launhardt then became its first Rector. He was a member of the Königliche Akademie des Bauwesens and the Preussische Herrenhaus, and was awarded an honorary degree from Dresden. His major work was therefore as a civil engineer. Nevertheless he published, in addition to the *Mathematical Principles of Economics*, a book on money entitled *Das Wesen des Geldes und des Wöhrungsfrage* (1985), which stressed the circular flow of income and the role of the velocity of circulation of money.

THE MATHEMATICAL PRINCIPLES AND ITS CRITICS

This book presents for the first time an English language edition of Launhardt's *Mathematische Begründung der Volkswirtschaftslehre* (1885). The first edition was reprinted in 1963, and several pages were translated in the anthology compiled by Baumol and Goldfeld (1968, pp. 28–30), but Launhardt's book has not previously been translated. The *Mathematical Principles of Economics* is a work of very high quality and contains many important and original contributions to economic theory. Indeed, it may claim to be one of Germany's most important contributions to neoclassical economic theory during the last quarter of the nineteenth century. In terms of mathematical economics, Launhardt can be regarded as the main successor in Germany of Thünen and Mangoldt, as Hutchison (1953, p. 186) has suggested. Yet he is nowhere near as well-known

1

as his fellow countrymen and the other pioneers of neoclassical economics. Launhardt also has a firm place in the important group of engineers who have made valuable contributions to economic theory, such as Dupuit, Ellet, Jenkin and others. Despite the fact that Launhardt's contributions cover a broader range of topics and are collected in a highly systematic form, the other engineers have received more recognition in the economics literature. It is hoped that this English edition will provide the basis of a significant re-evaluation of Launhardt's major work in economics.

It would, however, be much too simple to attribute the lack of appropriate recognition to the absence of an English translation. Blaug (1986, p. 123) has pointed out that, 'to anyone interested in the fascinating topic of multiple discoveries in science, and the associated questions of why some figures are systematically neg-lected, Launhardt's case affords a rich example'. Schumpeter has also commented, in the context of Launhardt's *Mathematical Princi-ples*, that 'it is curious to observe – and characteristic of the con-ditions in our field – that a type of research may be present and in full view and yet pass unnoticed' (1954, p. 851, n.15). No attempt can be made in this brief introduction to explore this issue in detail. However, it is worth mentioning that Launhardt's contribution was not only sadly neglected but was much maligned.

The most extensive criticism of Launhardt appeared in Wicksell's *Value, Capital and Rent* (1893, English edition, 1954), and was repeated in his *Lectures* (1901, English edition, 1934). In his intro-duction, Wicksell argued that Walras's 'German follower Laun-hardt, a skilled mathematician, presents Walras's principles in a simpler and more lucid form; but for the rest, Launhardt's work presents a striking example of the way in which a mathematical treatment of economic problems ought *not* to be carried out' (1934, p. 18). Wicksell's uncharacteristic hostility may perhaps have had something to do with Launhardt's criticism of Walras's comments on maximum utility, despite the fact that Wicksell acknowledged that Walras gave 'in several passages . . . a wrong or at least mislead-ing formulation' (1954, p. 19).

The issue concerns the difference between the competitive equili-brium and the allocation which maximizes total utility. Walras (1874, in 1954, p. 205) actually accused Gossen of confusing the two positions, then Launhardt accused Walras of a similar error, show-ing that the allocations were only the same under special conditions.

To add to the confusion, Wicksell strongly and incorrectly accused Launhardt of treating the special case as the general case; see Wicksell (1954, p. 76; 1934, p. 81, n.1). It is unfortunate that Samuelson later took Wicksell's argument at face value and stated that Launhardt's argument is 'mathematically and logically false. Yet he must be given credit for having made an attempt at rigor, and we can learn more from his unambiguous failure than from many pages of fuzzy literature effusion' (1947, p. 205). Wicksell's unjustified criticism of Launhardt seems to have had a strong influence on later views, yet a close comparison of the first section of *Value, Capital and Rent* (1954, pp. 17–96) with Launhardt's analysis of exchange, contained in Part 1 of the *Mathematical Principles*, shows the considerable extent to which Wicksell based his discussion on a simplified version of Launhardt, while adding the concept of the contract curve taken from Edgeworth.

The criticism has also been made of Launhardt that his analysis is severely restricted by the use of specific functional forms, in particular the use of a quadratic utility function. Wicksell (1954, p. 57) complained unjustly that Launhardt never attempted to defend the use of a quadratic function, and Fisher (1925, p. 119) suggested that although Launhardt's book contains 'some excellent things', it would have 'exhibited these excellencies better if the author had contented himself with solving problems in all their generality'. Schumpeter (1954, p. 948, n. 10) was more ambivalent, suggesting that, 'his almost ruthless use of particular forms of function – by which he produces results of disconcerting definiteness – should be studied and improved rather than condemned *a limine*'. It therefore seems worth stressing that Launhardt did indeed begin his analysis of most topics by taking completely general forms. When general results were exhausted, he used the specific forms for illustrative purposes but was careful to consider the robustness of his conclusions.

One important example of Launhardt's productive use of specific forms may be given here, concerning the 'equations of exchange'. Jevons had specified marginal utility as a function of quantities and recognized that his equations of exchange gave simultaneous equations, in terms of quantities exchanged, that are typically non-linear and thus difficult to solve. Walras used the familiar interpretation of the price ratio in terms of the ratio of quantities exchanged, and simply stated that the same equations could be solved to express quantities in terms of price ratios, without considering the method of solution or the conditions under which a solution would be available; his discussion suggests that he viewed them as linear equations. Launhardt, by assuming a specific functional form for utility functions, showed explicitly for the first time how demand functions could be derived from utility functions. He was then able to use the demand functions very effectively in a variety of contexts.

The use of specific functional forms is of course widespread in modern economic analysis. Launhardt's assumption was that the marginal utility of each good is a linear function of the quantity consumed of that good; it is a special case of the linear preference scale later used by Allen and Bowley (1935). It seems unfortunate that Launhardt has been criticized for examining special cases, particularly when the same type of criticism is not raised by those critics against other mathematical economists such as, for example, Cournot. Cournot's favourite approach when examining comparative statics was to take a Taylor series expansion, ignoring second-order and higher terms, thereby effectively assuming linear supply and demand curves.

THE STRUCTURE OF THE MATHEMATICAL PRINCIPLES

It has been suggested above that Launhardt's *Mathematical Principles of Economics* is a major contribution to neoclassical economics. Indeed its structure reflects very strongly the neoclassical emphasis on exchange as the central economic problem. Linked with that emphasis is the use of a utility analysis of constrained choice. Launhardt acknowledged the importance of Jevons's *Theory of Political Economy* (the second edition of 1879) along with Walras's *Mathematische Theorie der Preisbestimmung der Wirtschaftlichen Güter* of 1881. In a rather vague statement in the preface, Launhardt referred to his own independent discovery of a similar approach, but gave no details. There seems little point in speculation regarding subjective originality, however. What is clear is that Launhardt's mathematical skills, combined with strong economic insight, enabled him to go well beyond Walras and Jevons in the formal analysis of exchange.

The application of his utility analysis to the treatment of savings and interest, along with the supply of labour and its role in production, is also extremely impressive.

The structure of the book reflects the central role of exchange. Part 1 deals with the pure exchange model. This is notable for the explicit derivation of general equilibrium supply and demand curves (in a two-good model) from traders' utility functions, along with an analysis of exchange where a sequence of trades take place at disequilibrium prices. This part also contains Launhardt's careful treatment of maximum total utility and the distribution of the gains from exchange.

Part 2 is then concerned with the production of goods and the role of labour and capital. Consistent with the stress on the role of exchange, Launhardt concentrates on the supply of labour. His derivation of the individual supply curve, the treatment of aggregation problems, labour mobility in a general equilibrium framework and the role of intra-marginal rents is very impressive. It is of interest that after introducing money into the model, Launhardt at several points treats the marginal utility of money as constant, as Marshall was later to do, and as Jevons had suggested. The treatment of the demand for capital and its supply is also noteworthy, involving an analysis of savings and the rate of interest. It is perhaps surprising that Fisher (1930) later made no reference to this valuable contribution. Launhardt's discussion of the role of the entry and exit of firms in general equilibrium is also of interest.

The third and final part of the book turns to the transportation of goods and the location of industry, much of which had been published earlier, as Launhardt noted in his preface. This work, though neglected, was not surpassed until the 1930s. As Blaug (1986, p. 123) has argued, 'had his work been widely known, location theory might have saved itself roughly a quarter of a century in trying to integrate the demand side with the supply side in the analysis of the optimum location of business enterprises'. His contribution to location theory was thus highly original, as was his treatment of freight rates, in which Launhardt came extremely close to the marginal cost pricing rule. His assumption of constant average costs (so that marginal and average costs are equal) meant that, as Blaug (1986, p. 124) puts it, 'the marginal cost pricing rule failed to stand out in pristine clarity'.

The emphasis throughout the *Mathematical Principles* on the comparison of both competitive and monopoly outcomes with the arrangement that maximizes total utility, combined with the very broad range of topics considered, means that it would not be an exaggeration to describe Launhardt's book as the first systematic treatise on welfare economics.

THE TRANSLATION

The preparation of an English edition of the *Mathematical Principles* presents a number of difficult problems. The first and most obvious is that the late nineteenth-century German scientific style used by Launhardt is very complex; the sentences are very long and contain many subsidiary clauses. The approach adopted here was to begin with a fairly 'literal' translation. This was produced by Hilda Schmidt, who is neither a mathematician nor an economist. The resulting first draft was then edited to produce the present text. There is an enormous temptation facing an experienced editor to convert the literal translation into a smooth flowing English style that is much more succinct and easier to read. However, such an approach presents serious dangers. The editor may impose a greater clarity of expression and arrangement of the argument than may exist in the original. The argument may also be distorted by a desire to make it fit more closely a modern exposition of the economic problem being discussed. This temptation was therefore, as far as possible, resisted in the desire to produce a balance between accuracy and smoothness. There is then always a danger that the text will appear to be 'half German still', as Dalton (1923) said of McCabe's translation of the first edition of Cassel's *Theory of Social Economy*. But it was judged better to be guilty of this than to produce a text that resembles something the editor, rather than the original author, would have written.

There is one context where the introduction of more-modern terminology was thought to be appropriate, though not all readers will be expected to agree. Instead of using the expression 'usefulness equation', which occurs many times, the term 'utility function' was substituted. Similarly 'marginal utility' is used to describe a first (partial) derivative of the utility function. Frequent use was made by

Launhardt of the expression 'priceworthiness' to describe the ratio of marginal utility to price of a particular good; hence constrained utility maximization results in the equality of the 'priceworthiness' of all goods. This terminology has been retained below. Launhardt used many paragraphs consisting of only a single short sentence. It was decided in some places to group these sentences into single paragraphs.

The notation used by Launhardt also presents some problems. In particular, instead of using a superscript dash, such as the term p', or p'', Launhardt used p, or $p_{,,}$. Since this is rather awkward for the modern reader and potentially misleading, it was decided to use dashes in most cases. Exceptions were made where several parameters of a function were distinguished: hence $\alpha + \alpha_, x$ is written below as $\alpha + \alpha_1 x$, rather than $\alpha + \alpha' x$. Thus variables such as prices are distinguished using dashes, while parameters have subscript numbers, following a fairly standard convention in economics texts. Launhardt numbered some of his equations with the number on the left hand margin; the same numbering has been followed below, but numbers are placed in parentheses against the right margin. There is a slight inconsistency, in the original, in the use of lower- and upper-case letters for functions, particularly the utility function. Upper-case letters have been used throughout below.

Some of Launhardt's equations have many different 'layers' which must have presented problems for the typesetters. This often arises where, for example, the ratio of price p' to price p'' is printed as $\dfrac{p'}{p''}$ rather than (p'/p''). The latter approach has been adopted below where convenient. There are some fairly obvious misprints in the original equations, and these have been silently corrected. But these are minor; Launhardt's mathematics are accurate and clearly explained. The reader is told what is being done at each stage, and will typically only need a paper and pencil to fill in some of the stages where basic algebraic manipulations have been carried out. Anyone who has read Edgeworth (1881) will find Launhardt a model of clarity. Although Wicksell (1954) often simplified Launhardt's numerical examples, his explanations are more compressed and are easier to follow after reading Launhardt's original analysis.

Launhardt's diagrams were rather small, and none was given a title. The figures presented below are scaled reproductions of the original, but the temptation to add a descriptive title has been resisted.

NOTES AND FURTHER READING

For a discussion of the role of engineers in the history of economics, and further references, see Ekelund and Hebert (1983, pp. 271–5). Unlike Launhardt, large sections of Mangoldt's work have been translated into English (see Creedy, 1992, p. 46) and his work has been more widely discussed than that of Launhardt; on translations in economics see Creedy (1990). An Italian translation was made by Tullio Bagiotti in 1954. The last quarter of the nineteenth century has been described by Hutchison (1955) as a high point of cosmopolitanism in economics, yet Launhardt's work was seldom discussed. He is mentioned in passing by Antonelli (see Baumol and Goldfeld, 1968, p. 33) and approvingly by Pantaleoni (1898, pp. 77, 92, 132, 161, n.1, 255), but not by Pareto in his *Manuel*. There was no entry for Launhardt in the original *Palgrave's Dictionary*. Marshall actually deleted two references to Launhardt from later editions of his *Principles*; (see 1961, II, p. 247). Fisher briefly cites Launhardt in (1925, pp. 17, 88, 93, 100, 113) as well as making the critical comment quoted above, and lists several of his works in the bibliography of mathematical economics (1927, pp. 173–209). However, given Launhardt's discussion of savings and the rate of interest, it is curious that he is not mentioned in Fisher (1930). On his analysis of interest, see Niehans (1990, p. 292). He is not mentioned by Bowley (1924) nor in the bibliography compiled by Batson (1930), and is entirely ignored in the essays included in Hennings and Samuels (1990). An exception is Hutchison (1953, pp. 186–8), who corrects the error in Wicksell's criticism of Launhardt's discussion of maximum utility. Jaffé (1983, p. 91) simply dismissed Launhardt's analysis as 'irrelevant'.

Wicksell (1954, p. 53) criticized Launhardt for breaking the rule that 'economic truth must never be sacrificed to the desire for mathematical elegance'. He incorrectly suggested that Launhardt presented his results on repeated exchange as the general rule; see Wicksell (1954, p. 58). Wicksell (1954, p. 87) incorrectly stated that supply and demand curves similar to those drawn by Launhardt, in the back-to-back diagram with quantities related to the relative price, were in Mangoldt (1863). Furthermore, he does not really make it clear that the discussion in (1954, pp. 64–72) is taken from Launhardt. Wicksell's attitude to Launhardt is certainly curious. He also strongly criticized Jevons's concept of the 'trading body', though he was obviously not familiar with Edgeworth's (1881) analysis of the role of numbers in competition.

Schumpeter (1954, p. 948) suggests that the *Mathematical Principles* 'adopts the principles of Jevons and Walras, though we must accept Launhardt's claim to independent discovery "of a similar approach" since we have accepted the analogous claim of others. His treatment presents several original points that are all of them to its credit'. The back-to-back exchange diagram developed by Launhardt, and mentioned above, is considerably clearer than the exchange diagrams produced by Walras. What is surprising is that Walras's and Launhardt's diagrams have been so neglected in the secondary literature. Other than Wicksell's discussion, a very rare and brief discussion in the context of multiple equilibria, taken from Wicksell, is in Stigler (1965, p. 96). For extensive discussion of this device, see Creedy (1992).

On Launhardt's contribution to location theory, see Pinto (1977) and Niehans

(1990). Beckman and Thisse (1986) provide a survey of modern location theory which helps to place Launhardt's main results in perspective.

REFERENCES

Allen, R.G.D. and Bowley, A.L. (1935) *Family Expenditure*. London: P.S. King.

Batson, H.E. (1930) *A Select Bibliography of Modern Economic Theory 1870–1929*. London: George Routledge.

Baumol. W.J. and Goldfeld, S.M. (1968) *Precursors in Mathematical Economics: An Anthology*. London: London School of Economics.

Beckman, M.J. and Thisse, J.-F. (1986) 'The location of production activities'. In *Handbook of Regional and Urban Economics*, vol. 1, ed. P. Nijkamp. Amsterdam: North-Holland, pp. 21–95.

Blaug, M. (1986) *Great Economists before Keynes*. Brighton: Wheatsheaf.

Bowley, A.L. (1924) *The Mathematical Groundwork of Economics*. Oxford: Clarendon Press.

Creedy, J. (1990) 'Commentary on English-speaking pioneers in value and distribution theory.' In *Neoclassical Economic Theory*, ed. K. Hennings and W. Samuels. Boston: Kluwer, pp. 52–8.

Creedy, J. (1992) *Demand and Exchange in Economic Analysis: A History from Cournot to Marshall*. Aldershot: Edward Elgar.

Dalton, H. (1923) Review of *Theory of Social Economy*. *Economica*, pp. 223–6.

Edgeworth, F.Y. (1881) *Mathematical Psychics*. London: Kegan Paul.

Ekelund, R.B. and Hebert, R.F. (1983) *A History of Economic Theory and Method*. New York: McGraw Hill.

Fisher, I. (1925) *Mathematical Investigations in the Theory of Value and Prices*. New Haven: Yale University Press.

Fisher, I. (1927) 'Bibliography of mathematical economics.' In *Cournot's Researchers into the Mathematical Principles of the Theory of Wealth*, ed. I. Fisher. London: Stechert-Hafner, pp. 173–209.

Fisher, I. (1930) *The Theory of Interest*. New York: Macmillan.

Hennings. K. and Samuels, W. (eds) (1990) *Neoclassical Economic Theory 1870–1930*. Boston: Kluwer.

Hutchison, T.W. (1953) *A Review of Economic Doctrines 1870–1929*. Oxford: Clarendon Press.

Hutchison, T.W. (1955) 'Insularity and cosmopolitanism in economic ideas 1870–1914.' *American Economic Association Papers and Proceedings*, **45**, pp. 1–16.

Jaffé, W. (1983) *Essays on Walras*. ed. D.A. Walker. Cambridge: Cambridge University Press.

Mangoldt, H. (1863) *Grundriss der Volkswirtshaftslehre*. Stuttgart: Engelhorn.

Marshall, A. (1961) *Principles of Economics*. 9th (Variorum) edition, ed. C.W. Guillebaud. London: Macmillan.

Niehans, J. (1990) *A History of Economic Theory*. Baltimore: Johns Hopkins University Press.

Pantaleoni, M. (1898) *Pure Economics*, tr. T. Boston Bruce. London: Macmillan.

Pinto, J.V. (1977) 'Launhardt and location theory: rediscovery of a neglected book.' *Journal of Regional Science*, 17.

Samuelson, P.A. (1947) *Foundations of Economic Analysis*. Cambridge MA: Harvard University Press.

Schumpeter, J.A. (1954) *History of Economic Analysis*. London: Allen and Unwin.

Stigler, G.J. (1965) *Essays in the History of Economics*. Chicago: Chicago University Press.

Walras, L. (1874) *Elements of Pure Economics*, tr. (1954) W. Jaffé. London: Allen and Unwin.

Wicksell, K. (1934) *Lectures on Political Economy*, tr. E. Classen. London: Routledge.

Wicksell, K. (1954) *Value, Capital and Rent*, tr. S.H. Frowen. London: Allen and Unwin.

Mathematical Principles of Economics

Wilhelm Launhardt

Contents

Preface

The repeated attempts to treat economics mathematically have so far found little recognition. The negative position taken by authors writing on economics is probably mostly due to external circumstances, but can also be explained by referring to individual cases in which, due to one-sided or even false presuppositions, the mathematical treatment of economic questions has led to obviously incorrect results. In this context one could point to the formula of the natural wage developed by Thünen.

However, the antipathy towards a mathematical treatment of economics is to be lamented because the investigations of this science cannot be carried out in sufficient detail without the use of mathematical principles which are aimed at reaching the maximum impact with a minimum of input. It is widely accepted that mathematics represents nothing but the language which in strict reasoning depicts the relationship of measurable entities towards one another, something which cannot be expressed in ordinary language, or only in a very circumlocutory manner.

That indeed mathematics cannot explain in a satisfactory manner all aspects of economic problems, some of which lead into moral and political realms, must not be allowed to be a reason for condemning its application altogether or for sacrificing the help it alone has to offer.

The mathematical conception of economics proves to be of such benefit and versatility, even in a first attempt, that in writing this book I had to discipline myself in the strictest manner to keep my account as brief as possible, as a more extensive presentation of the subject would have led to discouraging proportions in the length of the material to be studied. For this reason I refrained throughout from drawing conclusions or applications of the developed formulae and from elaborating on side-issues which could conceivably restrict their general importance.

The importance of transport facilities and availability led me first towards experiments in a mathematical approach to questions of economics which were concluded in three essays, of which the first, entitled *Commercial Network Planning*, was published in 1872, the second entitled 'The most effective location of an industrial plant' appeared in *Zeitschrift des Vereins deutscher Ingenieure* (the *Journal of the Association of German Engineers*) 1882, and the last, under the heading of 'Economic questions of the railway system', 1883, appeared in the *Centralblatt der Bauverwaltung* (Central Papers of the Building Authorities). When, after these preliminary studies, I had grasped the task in its entirety, I learned about the work by two writers who had taken a similar direction before me. Their books were entitled *Mathematical Theory of the Determination of Prices of Economic Goods* by Leon Walras (in German by Ludwig von Winterfeld, Stuttgart 1881) and *The Theory of Political Economy* by Stanley Jevons (London 1879). In leaning on the works of both these scientists I have based my investigation on my schedule of the utility function and the deduction of equilibrium prices.

Two other books by Walras which have to be considered of great importance for the mathematical interpretation of economics have reached me, through the kindness of their author, only just before the completion of the printing of this book. These are the works *Théorie mathématique de la richesse sociale* (Lausanne 1883) and *Elements of Pure Economics* (Lausanne 1874 and 1877). The first contains the aforementioned theory of the formation of prices which was known to me through the German edition by L. von Winterfeld at the time of writing my own book. Despite much effort I could not obtain an earlier book, by Cournot, *Recherches sur les principes mathématiques de la théorie des richesses* (Paris 1838) until a few days ago when I found that this intelligent book had rested unread for almost half a century in the library of one of the larger German universities. Another book published a few years earlier by H.H. Gossen in Braunschweig with the title *The Laws of Human Interrelations*, which is supposed to deal with the mathematical reasoning of economics in exemplary fashion, seems to have disappeared altogether as I have been unable to locate it despite considerable effort.

As regrettably small as the success derived so far from the direction taken by the authors of these texts may seem, I find most decisive confirmation of my conviction that economics can become a fully accepted science in the fact, that entirely independent of each other, writers in Germany, Britain, France and Switzerland have undertaken the mathematical analysis of economics.

Hannover, 1 March 1885

WILH. LAUNHARDT

PART 1

The Exchange of Goods

1. Introduction

Everything that is suited to foster, improve or embellish human existence and to satisfy human needs, to increase the pleasure in living, to divert or lessen suffering, possesses *value*. The value forms the measure of the amount of effort which one would be prepared to make to attain the benefits or enjoyment of these things. Value is not inherent as such in goods, but consists of a relationship between the properties of goods and the person evaluating them, similar to a shadow not being a property of bodies, but an appearance depending on the shape of the bodies and the strength and position of the light source, or as the sound of a hunting horn is not its property, but depends on the construction of the instrument and the person blowing into it.

As the shape of the shadow varies depending on the location of the light source and the frequency of the sound must change depending on the speed of the entering airstream, even though the shape of one always depends on the shape of the body and the other on the construction of the horn, so too will the value of a thing vary in the opinion of the judge although the characteristics of the thing remain totally unchanged. The negro living in the tropics will attach a lower value to fuel and a warming fur coat, but a higher value to a cool drink or a sunshade than a Laplander at the edge of the Arctic sea. The value of a thing is not only measured according to which need it fulfils, but also according to the importance which the fulfilment of the need has for the judge. The demands which are made from different directions on the same thing can vary greatly and therefore lead to very different values. For instance the value of limestone for road works where its grade of hardness is particularly relevant will be estimated differently than in a situation where its use in the production of cement is considered where its chemical composition is most important.

It seems therefore after all that the definition or estimation of the value depends not only on the objective properties of the article in question, but also on the subjective opinion of the judge. Notwith-standing the variation which the results of the estimation of value will contain, the definition of the degree of value must be based on a certain unity. *The value of a thing is measured by the degree of effort the investment of which is considered proportionate to the effort necessary to possess a thing by the judge.* The natural unit to deter-mine the extent of value is therefore a certain measure of human effort or work, say the daily work-output of one person. The objec-tion that due to the variation in work-output by one or another person a definite unified measure cannot be established is to be answered with the fact that the height of the Cologne Cathedral remains unchanged whether it is measured by a German in metres or an Englishman in feet. The condition of making the correct assess-ment of the height is merely that each individual measures every-thing with a consistent measure. In place of the unit of the human work-output any other given natural unit of value indication can of course be used, e.g. money, in which this natural unit can be expressed. It can therefore be said that one hectolitre of wheat equals the value of the work-output of one person for five working days, and if the working day of one person is valued at two marks, it is worth ten marks; in contrast it cannot be said that the hectolitre of wheat is worth so many metres or kilograms; but perhaps it is worth 2,000,000 metre-kilograms as the mechanical human work-achieve-ment rate amounts to 400,000 metre-kilograms.

As the measure of value is based on a unit established by human labour, the determination of a value unit is possible only for such things whose possession can be achieved by a person through work. The value of good health, of favourable weather, the true affection of a friend etc. can therefore not be expressed in figures. In contrast to such things of value the securing of which is beyond the realm of the human will or at least does not completely depend on human effort, the things which can be obtained through human activity, are called *economic* goods.

It is the *science of economics* which is concerned with the ways and means through which possession of these economic goods can be achieved. It is the purpose of this science, as briefly and succinctly remarked by Courcelle-Seneuil, to investigate *how the enjoyment of economic goods can be achieved with a minimum of effort.*

The treatment and processes applied to economic goods between their origin and final consumption can be divided into three categories:

1. Processes which incorporate the *production of goods*. As a first step the *raw materials* provided by nature must be gained which occurs through agriculture, forestry, mining, hunting and fisheries. This is followed by a change, if the raw materials are not consumed in their original state, of their shape and content, their composition and disection to make them suitable for certain applications. This is the responsibility of the trades and crafts.
2. Processes which relate to a *change in location*.
3. Processes which are caused by a *change in the possession* of goods.

In accordance with these three processes economics can be divided into three sections in which, for the purpose of developing a scientifically reasoned order, the first, *barter or exchange of goods*, the second, *the production of goods*, and the third, the *distribution of goods*, are contained.

2. Consumption and Capital Goods

Economic goods are either *goods for consumption* which allow a single process of use and are destroyed or are at least useless for further processes of the same sort, or *goods for use* which allow repeated use and are affected by this process either not at all or lose their usefulness only after more or less frequent use for the same purpose. The indicative characteristic of goods for use, which can also be named *capital* (in the general sense of the word), is that *the sum of the benefit which can be derived from them is not used on one occasion but only in the course of time little by little. The value of this capital must therefore be measured in two directions, in the degree of enjoyment and period of usefulness, while the value of the consumption goods the enjoyment of which can take place only in a one-off situation, can be determined in one direction only, the degree of pleasure or enjoyment.*

When determining the value of the capital one very important circumstance must be kept in mind, that is, *the enjoyment will be estimated correspondingly lower the more distant is the time in which the benefit can be reaped.* The explanation for this can initially be sought in the degree of uncertainty which exists, whether the expected benefit will actually occur in the future or not. But even if the fullest surety were guaranteed, the uncertainty for the judge remains of whether his present ability to reap the benefits will remain the same in the future. Whether one considers this explanation as sufficient or not, the fact remains that *a pleasure or benefit guaranteed for the future rates lower than the same pleasure available at present.*

If an immediately usable benefit has the value g, an equal benefit, available only after the period t, will be estimated at the lower value of εg whereby ε describes a coefficient depending on period t which will always be lower than 1. The same benefit g would, if available only after two units of t have passed, when it is valued after the first period has elapsed so that until its due date only one more period t remains, would be estimated at εg, a present value of $\varepsilon^2 g$. Therefore, capital goods which give over n periods the benefit g each period have a present value of:

$$W = g(\varepsilon + \varepsilon^2 + \varepsilon^3 + \ldots \varepsilon^n).$$

As ε is smaller than 1, the series is convergent and its sum is:

$$W = g(\varepsilon - \varepsilon^{n+1})/(1 - \varepsilon).$$

Substituting the coefficient $\varepsilon = 1/(1 + i)$, which depends on the individual periods, it follows that:

$$W = \frac{g}{i}(1 - \frac{1}{(1+i)^n}). \tag{1}$$

If the capital is indestructable, which means that the number of cases of use is infinite, the result is:

$$W = g/i. \tag{2}$$

The extent of the use or benefit which is delivered by the capital in each period is called the *capital income* while the coefficient i is the *interest rate*. One can base the capital income and the interest rate on any period of time, but as a rule an annual period is chosen. According to (2): *the present value of capital of unlimited duration equals the capital income divided by the interest rate.* If therefore a loan or a block of land gives an annual income of 100 Marks and the interest is 0.05. the capital value is $W = 100/0.05 = 2000$.

The value deriving from capital of infinite duration may be called the *unlimited capital value.* If the duration of the capital is however limited to a number of years, n, the unlimited capital value must be multiplied by $\{1 - 1/(1 + i)^n\}$.

The interest is the compensation for waiting for the pleasure or for the temporary sacrifice of a pleasure. If a pleasure to which one is entitled immediately occurs only after a year, it must increase as a compensation by a multiple of $1 + i$. The pleasure to occur only after one year of waiting, $g(1 + i)$, has a present value of only g. Consumption goods can be used immediately, or, according to their ability to keep, can be used at a later date. The stored quantity of consumption goods used up over a period of time obtains through this the character of goods for use or of capital, but they do not turn into capital because the possibility remains to use up instantly the total of the pleasure offered by them. The decisive feature of capital is that its benefit or pleasure can be obtained only over a period of time.

A vineyard which supplies annually 10 hectolitres of wine is a form of capital which represents, based on annual interest of 5%, the same value as a wine supply of 200 hectolitres. The wine supply becomes equal to capital in value, but does not become capital in the real sense because, with the help of friends, it could be drunk in a single day. The goods falling into the category of capital are to be separated into four groups:

1. *Natural capital of infinite duration.* This is *real estate capital* as for example blocks of land, rivers.
2. *Natural capital of limited duration.* This is *possession of animals* as for example work horses, dairy cows, but most importantly the human worker.
3. *Artificial capital of infinite duration.* This is money.
4. *Artificial capital of limited duration.* This is property such as buildings, machinery, tools, clothing, furniture.

The use of some capital is ongoing as for example that of a river, or of habitation where one has to assume cases of usage as being infinitely small consecutive time periods. With other kinds of capital, usage takes place in consecutive periods of longer duration as is the case in the annual harvest of fields or forests. Finally, usage can occur in cases of use repeated on an irregular basis, as with tools. In such a case the value of the capital is increased by the speed with which the total use available has been extracted. A hammer is more valuable for the smith who uses it every day than for someone who only uses it for an occasional nail driven into a wall or to hammer shut the lid of a wooden box.

It is impossible to draw the border between consumption goods and capital in a precise manner as, strictly speaking, for the use of every kind of consumption good a certain investment of time is necessary. The iron glove of a knight surely was capital to him, with a coarse leather glove some doubt exists as to whether it represents a consumption or capital good, while ladies' delicate ball gloves made of kid leather are undoubtedly consumption goods.

The smaller is the number, n, of individual cases of usage, which is inherent in the capital in question, and the faster these cases of usage follow one another, the smaller i becomes, the closer the value determined in (1) comes to the figure, g, which represents the value of a single case of usage, that is the value of consumption goods.

3. The Utility Function

To satisfy human needs the consumption or use of a certain quantity of economic goods is necessary. The measure of satisfaction depends on the quantity of goods available for satisfaction, but does not grow in proportion to an increase in supply. A daily consumption of 500g of bread may ensure survival; by adding another 500g, nutrition will be improved; another 500g to 1000g will change it to ample supplies. But the increase in consumption above the measure of complete satisfaction must be detrimental. According to the usefulness of having been supplied with 500g of bread per day this will be greatly valued, the second 500g will be of less value, and a further increase in daily consumption quantities will be unwelcome.

As in this example by Stanley Jevons, all other economic goods will be valued in a similar fashion. For a dry lot of agricultural land the supply of water will be much welcomed; that is, the utility of the water supply will increase to a certain degree with the increase in the quantity supplied. As soon as the optimum quantity of water has been supplied, any additional irrigation would not only be without value, but would have a damaging effect. In *The Isolated State* Thünen gives another example. For working the land, a plough is of great value. For a farm of a certain size a certain number of ploughs, say 10, would be considered desirable. An additional plough which could be used in emergencies will be of lower value than the tenth; a twelfth plough may not be used at all because the available number of horses is sufficient only for eleven ploughs but it is still of a certain value, less than that of the eleventh, because it can be utilized when one of the other ploughs has broken down. But a fourteenth or fifteenth plough would be worthless for the farmer because these would more than likely never be used; they would present a useless piece of equipment which would even be disturbing because it infringes on the disposable storage space.

After these examples clearly no further proof is needed *that the utility or the value of goods or possessions does not increase in the*

Figure 1

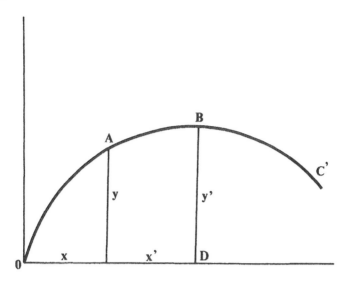

same ratio as an increase in quantity, but grows more slowly. The dependence of utility, y, on the quantity of goods, x, can therefore be expressed as a function:

$$y = F(x).$$

This is demonstrated in Figure 1, by OABC if the quantities of goods are entered as abscissas and the relevant units of utility as ordinates.

The exact determination of the shape of the *utility function* will present great difficulties even though it does not appear to be impossible to derive this for certain cases from suitable statistical observations. About the form of the utility function it is only known that for a quantity of goods x = 0 the utility is y = 0, that the utility grows more slowly than the quantity of goods, and for a certain quantity a maximum of utility is reached. A further increase in the quantity of the good will reduce utility.

Where, for the construction of examples or for the sake of clarity, the use of a certain form of the utility function appears necessary, F(x) will be accepted as a polynomial in x of which for approximation only the first two terms will be retained so that:

$$y = \alpha x - \alpha_1 x^2.$$

This approximate form fulfils everything that is known about the utility function in that for $x = 0$, and for $x = \alpha/\alpha_1$, y equals zero, and for $x = \alpha/2\alpha_1$ it reaches a maximum. This simple factual circumstance which is demonstrated through the *utility function* represents the only basis for scientific economics. Great efforts of deep thought were wasted to specify the concepts of *barter value*, *use value* and *price*. These concepts not only remained cumbersome and confused but were incorrect and wrong, because the basic truth underlying economics which is expressed in the utility function had not been recognized. The Swiss scientist Walras and the Englishman Stanley Jevons have earned the great merit of having been the first to express the truth deriving from the utility function.

The principle expressed through the utility function may be demonstrated once more by example. Imagine Robinson Crusoe on his island working to provide his food and fuel needs. Of the twelve hours available to him for work he uses eight hours to obtain eight pounds of fruit, and four to collect four bundles of firewood. He has recognized that in this manner, in accordance with the working power available to him, he can best provide for his food and fuel requirements. From this one could deduce that as Robinson spends one working hour both for collecting one pound of fruit and for gathering one bundle of firewood, one pound of fruit must be of equal value to him as one bundle of firewood. Why does Robinson not collect nine pounds of fruit and only three bundles of firewood? He will answer that he will have a little more to eat but will be short of fuel. This must mean that a bundle of firewood is of greater value than a pound of fruit. Would he then be better off gathering five bundles of firewood and seven pounds of fruit? Robinson will explain that even though he would feel warmer, he would not have enough to eat. Could it be that contrary to the earlier expressed opinion, a pound of fruit has after all a greater value than a bundle of wood?

The solution to these contradictions can easily be obtained from the utility function according to which not *every* pound of fruit has the same value as *every* bundle of firewood to Robinson, but only the eighth pound of fruit is equal to the fourth bundle of firewood. A ninth pound of fruit has a lower value for Robinson than the eighth, he therefore will not exchange it for the fourth bundle of firewood which is equal in value to the eighth pound of fruit. Looking at it the other way round, the fifth bundle of firewood is of a lower value to him than the fourth, so he will not be inclined to give his eighth pound of fruit for it.

It could be objected that the whole argument is only applicable to Robinson Crusoe living on his own in total seclusion, that in contrast to this in a larger economic society where one pound of fruit and one bundle of firewood each cost one working hour, both goods should always have the same value and can thus be exchanged for each other. But this would be a grave mistake. Those two goods could only be exchanged for each other if the total quantities of both goods were related to each other like eight to four.

For the assessment of the form of the utility function, according to which the value of a given quantity of goods is determined, it will have to be kept in mind that for the estimate of value, not only the quantity for immediate use is to be considered but also the storable quantity for future use. The quantity of goods will have, as detailed in Chapter 2, a utility y on its consumption but a present value of $y/(1 + i)^n$ if it is used only after n periods. In the coefficient i not only the ordinary interest needs to be considered but also the deterioration of value due to storage of the goods as well as the costs arising from the use of storage space. With correct distribution of the total quantity of goods over time, the last units must be of equal value to those in the present; because, if the last used unit had a lower utility than those used in earlier time periods, it would have been used wastefully and should have been used in a time unit in which it would have greater utility.

With this in mind the following formula has to be considered as arising from the utility function, $y = F(x)$, in order to bring forth from an increase in the quantity of goods of dx an increase in utility of dy. The utility:

$$\frac{dy}{dx} = F'(x)$$

which is added by another unit is called *the pressure of the last satisfied need* by Walras while Stanley Jevons has introduced the expression *degree of utility*. Both concepts for the first derivative of the utility function or for the tangent of the utility graph are far better than another expression *rarety* used by Walras.

The degree of utility is greatest for the first unit obtained of any goods; with the growth in the quantity of goods the utility also increases, but the degree of utility is lower. Finally if the quantity of goods has increased so much that an increase in utility through adding another unit of goods is not possible, that is if saturation has been reached, the degree of utility is zero. If the saturation point is passed, the utility decreases and the degree of utility becomes negative.

4. The Fundamental Law of Barter

If an owner of good A, the utility function of which is $y = F(x)$, owns a quantity a, and another owner of good B with a utility function of $y = \Phi(z)$, owns a quantity b, those two owners can exchange a certain quantity of their goods with each other and will do this to the extent to which they derive utility. Initially it may be supposed that the utility of both goods is estimated by the owners to be equal, in other words the value of the goods is based by both owners on the utility function for good A of $y = F(x)$ and for good B of $y = \Phi(z)$.

If in barter, p" units of good A are exchanged for p' units of good B, with x units of good A which are bartered for z units of good B, the result must be $z = (p'/p'')x$. The relative values p' and p" on which the barter is based are obviously nothing but the unit prices p' for good A and p" for good B measured on some sort of scale.

After the exchange the owner of A has retained of his initial good an amount $a - x$ and of the other good a quantity z, so that the utility of his possession is as follows:

$$N = F(a - x) + \Phi(z).$$

The value of x for which utility is a maximum is found by differentiating with respect to x and setting the result equal to zero. This gives: $-F'(a - x) + \Phi'(z)dz/dx = 0$,   and   as $z = (p'/p'')x$, $dz/dx = p'/p''$ and:

$$\frac{F'(a - x)}{\Phi'(z)} = \frac{p'}{p''}. \tag{3}$$

The Fundamental Law of Barter derives from this equation, which expressed in words is as follows: *For an owner the highest degree of utility of an exchange of goods is reached if the degrees of utility of the goods in his possession relate as do unit prices of the goods.*

Equation (3) can also be expressed as:

$$\frac{F'(a - x)}{p'} = \frac{\Phi'(z)}{p''}.$$

(4)

If one names the quotient of the degree of utility and the unit price the *priceworthiness* of the goods, then the fundamental law of barter can be expressed in the following manner: *For the owner, equality of priceworthiness must be achieved through an exchange of the goods in his possession.*

The correctness of this sentence can be understood without mathematical argument by simple reflection. The priceworthiness of goods indicates the degree of utility per unit price. If this measure were less for one of the goods than for the other, one would gain in pleasure if further quantities of the good for which the unit price gives less utility were exchanged for further quantities of the good which gives greater pleasure per unit price. The limit for the continuation of the exchange will be reached as soon as the degree of utility of both goods relative to the price per unit will be received.

For the second owner B the same conditions apply. He will have reached, after the exchange, a utility from his possessions which is equal to:

$$N = \Phi(b - x) + F(x).$$

By differentiating with respect to z the condition for the maximum is: $-\Phi'(b - z) + F'(x)\, dx/dz = 0$, and as $dx/dz = p''/p'$:

$$\frac{F'(x)}{\Phi'(b - x)} = \frac{p'}{p''}$$

(5)

or

$$\frac{F'(x)}{p'} = \frac{\Phi'(b - z)}{p''}.$$

(6)

However, the second owner will not always value goods A and B according to the same utility function as the first owner. If he estimates the utility of good A on $y = F(y)$ and the utility of good B not on $y = \Phi(z)$, but on $y = \psi(z)$, then the fundamental law of barter will be to him:

$$\frac{F'(x)}{\psi'(b - z)} = \frac{p'}{p''}$$

thus the same fundamental law of barter applies.

5. Supply of Goods

If from equation (3), which for the owner of good A offers the most favourable conditions for the barter against good B, x is obtained, the extent of *supply* is derived, that is the quantity of the goods which an owner at a given relative price of p'/p" has to exchange of his own possessions to derive a maximum of utility. If the relative price on which the exchange is based changes, the supply will also change. Supply is therefore a function of price, which is demonstrated in Figure 2 which shows the relative price as abscissas and the corresponding values of supply as ordinates.

Supply will be zero if the price of the offered good A is reduced to p^0, which is given by:

$$\frac{F'(a)}{\Phi(0)} = \frac{p^0}{p''}.$$

Only after the price of good A available for exchange rises above the

Figure 2

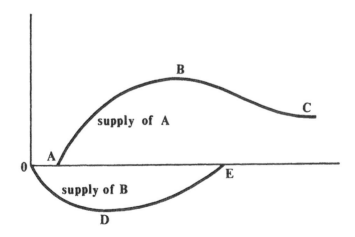

price, p^0, will the owner of A wish to exchange a quantity of his good, given in (3), for good B. This supply increases with the price p' until at a certain price a maximum supply is reached, because with a further increase in price the owner of A will receive a quantity of good B so large that a maximum of satisfaction is reached after only a small quantity of his highly priced good is made available. The graph of supply in Figure 2, depicted as the curve ABC, approaches the abscissa asymptotically from point B after having reached the maximum.

In order to obtain a more vivid idea of the shape of the *supply equation* and the *supply curve*, I shall introduce for the utility functions those approximations already referred to in Chapter 3. If for example

$$F(x) = \alpha x - \alpha_1 x^2$$

and

$$\Phi(z) = \beta z - \beta_1 z^2$$

that would mean that owner A, after having exchanged x of his good A for z of good B at a price ratio of p'/p'' has reached the following utility:

$$N = \alpha(a - x) - \alpha_1(a - x)^2 + \beta x p'/p'' - \beta_1(p'/p'')^2.$$

For maximum utility, differentiate with respect to x to give:

$$-\alpha + 2\alpha_1(a - x) + \beta p'/p'' - 2\beta_1 x (p'/p'')^2 = 0$$

from which the supply becomes:

$$x = \frac{\beta p'/p'' - (\alpha - 2\alpha_1 a)}{2(\alpha_1 + \beta_1(p'/p'')^2)}. \tag{7}$$

This supply will be zero for

$$p'/p'' = (\alpha - 2\alpha_1 a)/\beta \tag{8}$$

and the maximum for

$$\frac{p'}{p''} = \frac{\alpha - 2\alpha_1 a}{\beta} + \left\{ \left(\frac{\alpha - 2\alpha_1 a}{\beta} \right)^2 + \frac{\alpha_1}{\beta_1} \right\}^{0.5}. \qquad (9)$$

Equation (8) can also be expressed as:

$$\frac{\beta}{p''} = \frac{\alpha - 2\alpha_1 a}{p'}.$$

As β/p'' represents the priceworthiness of the first unit exchanged for good B. $\alpha - 2\alpha_1 a$ represents the marginal utility and therefore $(\alpha - 2\alpha_1 a)/p'$ shows the priceworthiness of the last unit of good A spent on obtaining the first unit of good B, thus the equation indicates: The supply of good A begins as soon as the priceworthiness of the last unit of this good equals the priceworthiness of the first unit of good B available for exchange.

If numbers are used and one takes a $= 400$, $\alpha = 1$, $\alpha_1 = 1/1000$, and b $= 480$, $\beta = 1.8$, $\beta_1 = 1/800$, the supply equals

$$x = \frac{3600\,p'/p'' - 400}{4 + 5\,(p'/p'')^2}. \qquad (10)$$

According to this, supply begins at a relative price of $p'/p'' = 1/9$, for which it is zero, reaches the maximum at a relative price of 1.0124, that is, an amount of 356. For a relative price of 2. supply would be 283, and for 10 reduce to 71, however becoming zero only after $p'/p'' = \infty$. With an infinitely high price for good A one has to supply only an infinitely small quantity of it to receive an infinitely large quantity of good B.

For the second proprietor B conditions under which he offers his good develop much in the same way. If he has given from his supply z and exchanged it for zp''/p' of good A, so his utility is:

$$N = \beta(b - z) + \beta_1(b - z)^2 + \alpha z p''/p' - \alpha_1 z^2 (p''/p')^2.$$

This becomes a maximum for:

$$z = \frac{\alpha p''/p' - (\beta - 2\beta_1 b)}{2\alpha_1(p''/p')^2 + \beta_1}$$

or if numerator and denominator are multiplied by p'^2/p''^2,

$$z = \frac{\alpha p'/p'' - (p'/p'')^2(\beta - 2\beta_1 b)}{2(\alpha_1 + \beta_1(p'/p'')^2)}.$$ (11)

Thus supplies become zero when:

$$\frac{\alpha}{p'} = \frac{\beta - 2\beta_1 b}{p''}$$

that is, if the priceworthiness of the first unit of good A to be bartered for good B corresponds to the unit of good B to be exchanged. The supply turns to zero for $p'/p'' = 0$, that is when supply is maximum, the price. p'', of good B is infinitely large compared to the price, p', of good A. Supply is a maximum for a relative price of:

$$\frac{p'}{p''} = \frac{-\alpha_1(\beta - 2\beta_1 b)}{\beta_1 \alpha} + \left\{ \frac{\alpha_1^2}{\beta_1^2}\left(\frac{\beta - 2\beta_1 b}{\alpha}\right)^2 + \frac{\alpha_1}{\beta_1} \right\}^{0.5}.$$

In Figure 2 supplies z are depicted according to (11) for various quantities of the relative price, p'/p'', of good B entered as ordinates below the axis of abscissas and represented by curve ODE. Using the numerical values:

$$z = \frac{2000\, p'/p'' - 1200\, (p'/p'')^2}{4 + 5\, (p'/p'')^2}$$ (12)

which is zero for $p'/p'' = 0$ and $1\frac{2}{3}$, however for 0.535 reaches a maximum amount of 157.

6. Demand

If equation (5), which has established the most favourable conditions for trader B for the barter of his good A, is solved for x, one arrives at the quantity of good A which can be exchanged by trader B most favourably, that is to reach a maximum of benefit, with a price ratio of p'/p". This is the extent of the *demand* for the good A. The demand is naturally greatest when the price p' of good A equals zero and will reach $\alpha/2\alpha_1$ when saturation develops when the degree of utility $F'(x) = 0$. The higher is the price p' compared to price p" of good B, the smaller is the demand, until finally it is zero when:

$$\frac{p'}{p''} = \frac{F'(0)}{\Phi'(b)}$$

that is for

$$\frac{\Phi'(b)}{p''} = \frac{F'(0)}{p'}$$

when the priceworthiness of the first available unit of good A is as large as the last unit of good B available for exchange.

If demand is depicted as ordinates to the abscissa measuring the price ratio p'/p" the locus of these ordinates determine the *demand curve* as is demonstrated in Figure 3 as FGH. For better demonstration we may, as in the case of the supply curve, base the demand curve on the utility function. If trader B has exchanged a quantity $z = (p'/p'')x$ of his good for x of good A he will have reached utility of

$$N = \beta(b - xp'/p'') - \beta_1(b - xp'/p'')^2 + \alpha x - \alpha_1 x^2$$

which will reach a maximum for

$$x'' = \frac{\alpha - (\beta - 2\beta_1 b)p'/p''}{2\{\alpha_1 + (p'/p'')^2/\beta_1\}}. \tag{13}$$

39

Figure 3

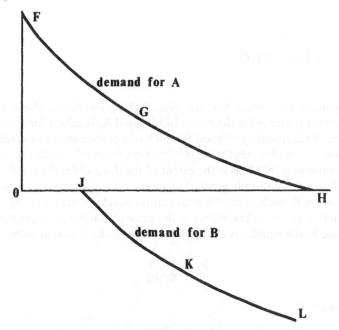

This demand will turn to zero for

$$\frac{p'}{p''} = \frac{\alpha}{\beta - 2\beta_1 b}.$$

For the earlier assumed values, the following demand is reached:

$$x'' = \frac{2000 - 1200(p'/p'')}{4 + 5\,(p'/p'')^2} \tag{14}$$

which reaches its highest point of 500 when $p'/p'' = 0$, and is zero for $p'/p'' = 5/3$.

The demand of trader A for good B is found in the same way. If he has exchanged a quantity $x = (p''/p')\,z$ for z of good B his utility is:

$$N = \alpha(a - zp''/p') - \alpha_1(a - zp''/p')^2 + \beta z - \beta_1 z^2$$

which will reach its maximum for:

$$z'' = \frac{\beta - (p''/p')(\alpha - 2\alpha_1 a)}{2\{\alpha_1(p''/p')^2 + \beta_1\}} \tag{15}$$

$$= \frac{\beta(p'/p'')^2 - (p'/p'')(\alpha - 2\alpha_1 a)}{2\{\alpha_1 + (p'/p'')^2 \beta_1\}}.$$

The demand commences when:

$$\frac{p'}{p''} = \frac{\beta}{\alpha - 2\alpha_1 a}$$

and steadily increases the more p'/p'' grows, and approaches asymptotically the value $\beta/2\beta_1$ with which saturation of good B has been established. The demand curve of trader A for good B is depicted in Figure 3 by the line JKL. Using the numerical values as an example the result is:

$$z'' = \frac{3600 (p'/p'')^2 - 400 p'/p''}{4 + 5(p'/p'')^2} \tag{16}$$

which will turn into zero for $p'/p'' = 1/9$ and with an increasing price ratio approaches asymptotically the figure 720, the quantity of good B for which complete saturation occurs.

7. Equality of Supply and Demand: Equilibrium Prices

In Figure 4 the supply and demand curves of good A are above the abscissa and those for good B below it. If the price ratio p'/p" is small, then the demand for the low-priced good A is large; this is however not offered at all at a low price so that no exchange can take place. Only after the price rises to p' = (1/9) p" is good A offered in small quantities, and is still in strong demand but not as strongly as

Figure 4

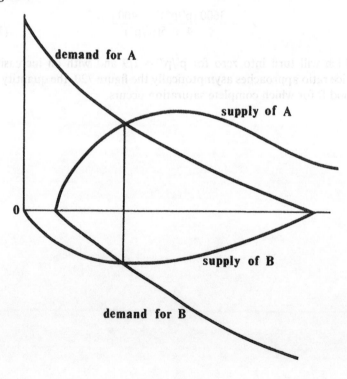

previously. With a growing price ratio the supply of good A increases, but the demand decreases until at a certain price ratio demand and supply will be in balance, a situation depicted at the point of intersection of the supply curve with the demand curve. In the market place the price of the good demanded will rise, as long as demand is not satisfied by supply; as soon as supply exceeds demand, a fall in the price for the good in question will occur. The battle over the price will cease only after supply and demand are equally strong. The prices resulting from such a situation are called *equilibrium prices* by Walras. The condition for equilibrium prices is reached when equations (3) and (5) coincide:

$$\frac{F'(a-x)}{\Phi'(z)} = \frac{F'(x)}{\Phi'(b-z)}. \tag{17}$$

Equilibrium develops when equations (8) and (13) coincide, in the case of the supply and demand of goods A, or by (11) and (15) coinciding which indicate supply and demand for goods B:

$$\frac{p'}{p''} = \frac{\alpha - \alpha_1 a}{\beta - \beta_1 b} \tag{18}$$

from which, for the numerical example, the result is $p'/p'' = 1/2$. In equilibrium, a quantity $x = 266$ of good A is exchanged for a quantity $z = 133$ of good B.

Trader A has achieved, after the exchange, a balanced priceworthiness:

$$\frac{\alpha - 2\alpha_1(a-x)}{p'} = \frac{\beta - 2\beta_1 z}{p''}$$

which in the case of the assumed values equals $1.466/p''$. Trader B achieves

$$\frac{\alpha - 2\alpha_1 x}{p'} = \frac{\beta - 2\beta_1(b-z)}{p''}.$$

It is simple to prove that in an exchange at equilibrium the sum of the utility for both proprietors, that is the utility achieved in an overall economic sense, has reached a maximum. The sum is:

$$N = F(a - x) + \Phi(z) + F(x) + \Phi(b - z).$$

The prerequisite for reaching the maximum is:

$$\frac{dN}{dx} = -F'(a - x) + \Phi'(z)\frac{dz}{dx} + F'(x) - \Phi'(b - z)\frac{dz}{dx} = 0$$

or, as $dz/dx = p'/p''$

$$\frac{F'(a - x) - F'(x)}{\Phi(z) - \Phi'(b - z)} = \frac{p'}{p''}. \tag{19}$$

This equation is complete as soon as equations (3) and (5) simultaneously coincide, that is when equilibrium exists. This important truth was discovered quite independently of the form of the utility function, showing that a maximum of utility is achieved if the exchange takes place at equilibrium prices, where supply and demand are equal. This truth, together with the fact that in the price battle in the market place the balance between supply and demand must undoubtedly be reached, leads to the conclusion that *by the natural effects of the free movement of competition, by 'laissez faire, laissez passer', the common good will be achieved in the surest way.* But in this conclusion lies a grave error at which *Walras*, too, arrived in his otherwise so ingenious explanation, as will be proven in the research to follow.

8.   Gain through Exchange

Trader A who possessed prior to the exchange a utility F(a) has obtained after the exchange a utility of $F(a - x) + \Phi(z)$; that is, utility gained by the exchange is:

$$G' = F(a - x) - F(a) + \Phi(z)$$

while the gain of trader B is as follows:

$$G'' = \Phi(b - z) - \Phi(b) + F(x).$$

Without knowledge of the form of the utility function, the extent of these gains cannot be proved. If the utility functions are based on the approximations $F(x) = \alpha x - \alpha_1 x^2$ and $\Phi(z) = \beta z - \beta_1 z^2$, then:

$$G' = \beta z - (\alpha - 2\alpha_1 a)x - \alpha_1 x^2 - \beta_1 z^2 \qquad (20)$$

$$G'' = \alpha x - (\beta - 2\beta_1 b)z - \alpha_1 x^2 - \beta_1 z^2. \qquad (21)$$

If $z = (p'/p'')x$, the resulting gain for both proprietors, at equilibrium prices $\dfrac{p'}{p''} = \dfrac{\alpha - \alpha_1 a}{\beta - \beta_1 b}$, if the quantity exchanged is obtained from (7) or (13) is for both:

$$G = \frac{\{a\,\alpha_1(\beta - \beta_1 b) + b\beta_1(\alpha - \alpha_1 a)\}^2}{4\{\alpha_1(\beta - \beta_1 b)^2 + \beta_1(\alpha - \alpha_1 a)^2\}}. \qquad (22)$$

The truth of the statement that *in an exchange at equilibrium both owners gain equal amounts*, is only proved in the case where the utility function is of the form accepted as approximately correct. Using the numerical values proprietor A owned prior to the exchange property giving a utility of $400 - 4000^2/1000 = 240$, which is increased by the exchange to 333, that is increased by 93; in contrast trader B has increased the utility of his property by way of

45

the exchange from 576 to 669, that is also increased it by 93. With an exchange at equilibrium prices therefore the poor proprietor gains the same amount as the rich proprietor, relative to his former property even more. For the example the gain of the poorer trader A amounts to approximately 39 percent, that of the richer trader B to only 16 percent.

Even though it was proved in Chapter 7 that through an exchange at equilibrium prices the sum of the gain by both proprietors is the maximum, that is for the common good the exchange at equilibrium prices is most favourable, nevertheless the exchange at equilibrium prices does not necessarily represent equally favourable results for the two proprietors. If this were the case the battle for prices would be a silly and unnecessary effort; there would prevail in the market place friendly cooperation between sellers and buyers to establish the equilibrium prices. In fact, however, each trader will obtain a higher gain if he does not go down to the equilibrium price, but maintains instead a higher price. Although he will be unable to sell the entire quantity of goods that he offers and therefore the number of units exchanged is lower than at equilibrium prices, the gain on each unit will be greater to the extent that the overall gain will be greater than in an exchange at equilibrium prices.

According to (21) the gain of trader A, after having exchanged z units of the foreign good for x units of his own good will be as follows, when it is considered that $z = (p'/p'')x$:

$$G' = \{\beta(p'/p'') - \alpha + 2\alpha_1 a\}x - \{\alpha_1 + \beta_1(p'/p'')^2\}x^2.$$

The proof of the fact to be explained becomes simplest and clearest when certain values are introduced. In accord with the values adopted earlier, the following results:

$$G' = (1.8\,(p'/p'') - 0.2)\,x - (\frac{1}{1000} + \frac{1}{800}\,(p'/p'')^2)x^2.$$

When the demand, x, from the price ratio p'/p'', is entered according to (14), the result is:

$$G' = \frac{-2520\,(p'/p'')^2 + 5040\,(p'/p'') - 1400}{4 + 5\,(p'/p'')^2}.$$

This gain of utility reaches its maximum for $p'/p'' = 0.78$, that is

$G' = 142$. With this price ratio, the most favourable for trader A, which results from introducing this into (14), 151 units of good A are exchanged for 118 units of good B. Trader B gains in this exchange only $G'' = 40$, as can be seen from introducing the exchanged quantities into (21). These calculations demonstrate that it is inadvisable for trader A to go down to the equilibrium price $p' = 0.5p''$ in which case he gains only 93, but to hold on to the higher price $p' = 0.78p''$ in which case his gain will be 142. In an overall economic sense the exchange at equilibrium prices would be more favourable because in such a case both proprietors together would gain 186 while the sum of the gain of both proprietors would be only $142 + 40 = 182$ in an exchange most favourable for proprietor A.

The second proprietor B will for his part work to achieve an exchange at a different price. In accord with (21), when using the numerical example, his gain will be:

$$G'' = \{1 - 0.6\,(p'/p'')\}\,x - \{\frac{1}{1000} + \frac{1}{800}\,(p'/p'')^2\}x^2.$$

If trader B pays a price lower than the equilibrium price, then the supply of good A will be smaller. If the supply of good A from (10) is entered, then

$$G'' = \frac{-5400\,(p'/p'')^2 + 4560\,(p'/p'') - 440}{4 + 5\,(p'/p'')^2}$$

for which a maximum will be obtained when $p'/p'' = 0.43$, that is $G'' = 106$. As can be deduced from (10), at this price 233 units of good A are exchanged for 100 units of good B.

If trader B, instead of going down to the equilibrium price $p' = 0.5\,p''$, is satisfied to exchange the available quantity of good A at the lower price $p' = 0.43\,p''$, he will obtain a gain of 106 instead of a gain of 93 which is obtainable at the equilibrium price. In this exchange owner A receives a gain of only 67 in accord with equation 20, so that the sum of the gain for both traders is $106 + 67 = 173$, that is the gain is reduced by 13 compared to an exchange at equilibrium prices.

These calculations prove that *the economically most favourable equilibrium prices by no means correspond to the prices most favourable to the individual trader.*

The prices which are sought by individual traders to their personal advantage differ widely; they compare in the battle over prices to the initial tactical positions taken up by opponents from which the battle commences. The victory in the battle over prices depends on the expertise, skill, toughness and staying-power of the fighters.

The proof of the fact that the traders earn their greatest profits at prices which differ from equilibrium prices as well as each others' has been established so far only in one particular example. But the figures are introduced merely to clarify matters, because the proof by way of the approximation formulae of the utility functions leads to lack of clarity of expression, as can be seen in equation (22). Even though the proof for every form of the utility function cannot generally be produced, it can nevertheless be easily achieved for any form of the utility function which corresponds to the one fundamental condition that utility increases more slowly than the increase in the quantity of goods and that it reaches a maximum at a certain quantity of goods.

Not before the end of Chapter 10 will I return to the remarkable facts which arise from these last calculations – that in an exchange at prices most favourable for the individual owner the economic gain, the sum of the gain for both owners, is smaller than in an exchange at equilibrium prices, and further, that this economic gain is smaller when the richer owner buys at the price most favourable for him than when the poorer owner succeeds in this.

9. Repeated Exchange

So far it has been recorded that the exchange takes place in a single business transaction. If this exchange takes place at a disequilibrium price, a balance between supply and demand has not been achieved, so calm has not yet been established in the market place. The victor who sold at a high price, and offered supplies which were not exhausted by demand, retains the option to lower his price and thus create new demand and so enter into a second exchange which produces further gain.

If trader A had exchanged a quantity a' of his original supply, a, for b' of good B, he will gain if he now exchanges x units of his goods for z units of good B:

$$G' = F(a - a' - x) + \Phi(b' + z).$$

This will, as $z = (p'/p'')x$, be a maximum for:

$$\frac{F'(a - a' - x)}{\Phi'(b' + z)} = \frac{p'}{p''}.$$

After introducing the approximation for the utility function, the result will be, solving for x:

$$x' = \frac{(p'/p'')(\beta - 2\beta_1 b') - (\alpha - 2\alpha_1(a - a'))}{2(\alpha_1 + \beta_1(p'/p'')^2)}. \tag{23}$$

The other trader B receives after this second exchange a profit of:

$$G'' = F(a' + x) + \Phi(b - b' - z)$$

which will be a maximum at:

$$\frac{F'(a' + z)}{\Phi'(b - b' - z)} = \frac{p'}{p''}.$$

49

from which the demand for good A can be obtained after introducing the approximation for the utility function, giving:

$$x'' = \frac{\alpha - 2\alpha_1 a' - \{\beta - 2\beta_1(b - b')\}(p'/p'')}{2(\alpha_1 + \beta_1 (p'/p'')^2)}. \tag{24}$$

By equating supply with demand, the equilibrium price ratio at which this second exchange takes place is:

$$\frac{p'}{p''} = \frac{\alpha - \alpha_1 a}{\beta - \beta_1 b}.$$

The final settling between supply and demand at equilibrium prices will occur even when the exchange is not affected in a single exchange transaction but in repeated transactions at varying prices as is otherwise achieved in a single transaction of exchange.

In the chosen example, trader A would be able to engage, after having carried out the first exchange at the price of $p'/p'' = 0.78$, in a second exchange at the equilibrium price of $p'/p'' = 0.5$ when he would in accordance with (23) and (24) be able to exchange once again 96 units of his goods for 48 units of goods B, achieving a gain in utility amounting to 154 compared to the level of his original property, while his opponent would have gained only 52 by his exchange transactions. It is most remarkable that in the course of these repeated exchange transactions the economic overall gain which amounts to $154 + 52 = 206$ is higher than would occur in a single transaction at equilibrium prices with which both owners together gained only 186.

If the first exchange had taken place to the advantage of the richer proprietor at a price ratio of $= 0.43$, then in a second transaction at the equilibrium price of $= 0.5$, 42 units of good A could have been exchanged for 21 units of good B, so that at the completion of both transactions owner B would have gained 109 and owner A gained 69. The economic gain in this instance would drop where the richer owner had succeeded in imposing his price, namely $109 + 69 = 178$ below the amount of 186 which was gained in a single exchange transaction. These calculations allow for the important fact to emerge that the rule proven in Chapter 7 according to which *an exchange at equilibrium prices achieves the greatest economic gain, is correct only under the condition that the exchange takes place in a single transaction*, but not when the balance between supply and demand takes place in several consecutive transactions at different prices.

These calculations demonstrate that, when the balance between supply and demand is based on prices which favour the poorer owner, not only his own but the total economic gain is higher than in a situation where the formulation of prices favours the wealthier trader. This important fact will be further explored in the following research.

10. Exchange at Changing Prices

If an equilibrium between demand and supply has not been achieved in an exchange at a given price, the owner whose supply was not exhausted by demand will decrease the price of his good to create new demand, or the owner whose demand was not met by supplies will decrease the price of his own good – a situation which equals a price increase for the other goods. These price changes will occur in reality not steadily but erratically by way of larger and smaller price rises or falls. The gain achieved in the exchange will, however, vary most from the amount gained in a single exchange at equilibrium prices when prices come close to equilibrium prices through minimal price changes and the price range begins at one of the two points where demand for one of the goods commences so that before reaching equilibrium prices countless extremely small exchanges have taken place. At every one of these transactions the owner whose demand is increased through infinitely small changes of the price by an infinitely small amount and who satisfies this increase of demand by way of an exchange will, in this circumstance, neither gain nor lose, so that after completion of the series of exchange transactions when reaching equilibrium prices the utility of the property held by him remains at the same level as before the start of the exchange transactions. The other owner who commences with his price at the borderline at which the first demand from his opponent occurs, gains with every one of the infinitely small exchange transactions. This situation will be further explained with sample figures.

Owner A whose good has a utility function of $y = x - x^2/1000$ gives away a utility of $dy = (1 - x/500)dx$ with a quantity of dx; that is, with the last differential of his stock amounting to 400, $dy_0 = 0.2dx$. Of good B whose utility equation is $u = 1.8z - z^2/800$, the differential has the utility $du = (1.8 - z/400)dz$; that is, the first differential which owner A obtains for the last differential of his goods $du_1 = 1.8dz$. The demand of owner A for good B will therefore commence as soon as the price ratio p'/p'' is larger than $1/9$; that is, when dz is larger than $(1/9)dx$. If owner A exchanges, at this borderline price, dx of his good for dz of good B, the gain will equal zero. Opponent B loses the utility of his last differential of his good $b = 480$; that is, $du = 0.6\,dz$, and receives for it the utility of the first differential of good A, that is, $dy_1 = dx$; that means he gains $dg = dx_1 - du_1$, meaning $dg = 8.4\,dz$ as $dz = (1/9)\,dx$. If the price ratio p'/p'' grows a little above $1/9$, a new demand by trader A for good B is created by the satisfaction of which once more only owner B will profit. If after a series of exchanges a quantity a_1 of good A is exchanged for b_1 of good B, the owner A has reached the following utility:

$$N' = \alpha(a - a_1) - \alpha_1(a - a_1)^2 + \beta b_1 - \beta_1 b_1^2$$

which must correspond to the initial utility of his property, and must equal $\alpha a - \alpha_1 a^2$, so that:

$$\beta b_1 - \beta_1 b_1^2 - \alpha_1 a_1 + 2\alpha_1 a a_1 - \alpha_1 a_1^2 = 0. \tag{25}$$

But equal priceworthiness must be reached:

$$\frac{\beta - 2\beta_1 b_1}{p''} = \frac{\alpha - 2\alpha_1(a - a_1)}{p'}$$

from which it can be concluded that the level of equilibrium prices has to be

$$\frac{p'}{p''} = \frac{\alpha - \alpha_1 a}{\beta - \beta_1 b},$$

hence:

$$\frac{\beta - 2\beta_1 b_1}{\beta - \beta_1 b} = \frac{\alpha - 2\alpha_1(a - a_1)}{\alpha - \alpha_1 a}. \tag{26}$$

Equations (25) and (26) determine the exchanged quantities of goods a_1 and b_1 according to which the gain obtained by proprietor B amounts to:

$$N'' = \alpha a_1 - \alpha_1 a_1^2 - \beta b_1 + 2\beta_1 b b_1 - \beta_1 b_1^2. \tag{27}$$

When introducing the earlier examples one arrives at an exchange, where a continuously changing price prevails, of $a_1 = 297$ versus $b_1 = 87$. Proprietor A is left without gain and proprietor B's gain is 147. If the price had commenced at the opposite end from a formula where for owner B the first demand for good A developed and he had under continuously changing prices satisfied his demand little by little, he would have remained without any gain. The exchange quantities are then arrived at by equating with zero, equation (27) and from equation (26). This gives $a_1 = 223$ and $b_1 = 203$, where A arrives at a gain of 220.

Compared with a single exchange at equilibrium prices in which each proprietor gains 93 and therefore an economic gain of 186 is achieved, it is possible in an extreme borderline case in which the price gradually approaches the equilibrium price, that one of the proprietors makes a greater profit while the other gains nothing. In this case the poorer proprietor can increase his gain to 220 while the richer proprietor gains only 147; this means that the economic gain is also variable depending on the success of one or the other proprietor within these loose parameters.

The outcome of the fight over the price depends decidedly on the skill and power of endurance of the individual proprietor. The assertion that *the unimpeded rule of free competition, laisser faire, must always lead to the most favourable solution for the common good, can therefore be called nothing but erroneous.*

The fact earlier emphasized, that *if the poorer is successful in regulating the price to his advantage, the economic gain in total for both proprietors engaged in an exchange is greater than in the case where the richer governs the formation of prices*, is of special importance. If proprietor B had, instead of a quantity of goods $b = 480$, only $b = 100$, representing a utility of only $(1.8)(100) - 100^2/800 = 167.5$ so that he is, contrary to our earlier supposition, poorer than A whose utility with supplies $a = 400$ amount to 240, he could, at continuously varying prices until they reached equilibrium prices of $p'/p'' = 24/67$, exchange $a_1 = 202$ units for $b_1 = 47$ and would gain 86, while the richer proprietor A would end up without profit. If however the richer proprietor A were in a position to manipulate prices in constant variation to his advantage, he would exchange $a_1 = 182$ for $b_1 = 90$ and gain in this process after all only 82, while B would finish up without any profit.

The 'right of the stronger', or more correctly, the law in accordance with which the stronger pushes over the weaker, manifests itself in a most decided manner everywhere in economic life. *Principles such as laisser faire, proposed by Manchesterdom for economic life, mean nothing else than to expose the weaker to the mercy of the stronger.* It is however not only the precept of justice which obliges civilized society to protect the weaker, but, as proved so far for the exchange of goods, it serves the common good in the best way. If justice demands that the exchange of goods is to be arranged in such a way that the total exchange of goods takes place without intermediate steps in a single transaction at equilibrium prices, in which both proprietors involved in the exchange obtain equal profit, then in consideration of the common good, it is necessary to assist the poorer proprietor to enable him initially to hold on to a higher price and only little by little go down to the level of the equilibrium price. Obviously this does not represent the robbing of the richer because in the extreme, practically impossible borderline case in which the total exchange is dissolved into an infinite series of exchange transactions, the richer owner, even if without profit, would not suffer any damage to his initial property level.

How far it is possible in an enlightened economic policy to regulate the formation of prices for the exchange of goods is a question which cannot be debated here. The intention was merely to prove that *by way of an unbridled to and fro of free enterprise, the laisser faire attitude, neither the demands of justice nor of the common good are served.*

11. Exchange of Two Goods Among Many Persons

If a total quantity a of good A is distributed among a large number n of owners in individual quantities of a_1, a_2 and a_n, the total quantity b of good B among m owners in individual quantities of b_1, b_2 to b_m, and if the owners of good A exchanged the quantities x_1, x_2 to x_m in the ratio $x_1(p'/p'')$, $x_2(p'/p'')$ and so on for good B, and further the owners of good B exchanged the quantities z_1, z_2 to z_m of their goods for $z_1(p''/p')$, $z_2(p''/p')$ and so on for good A then each owner must own quantities of goods of equal priceworthiness so that, at the time when both goods have reached an equal level of priceworthiness, the following equations are obtained:

$$\frac{F'(a_i - x_i)}{p'} = \frac{\Phi'(x_i p'/p'')}{p''}, \; i = 1,n$$

$$\frac{\Phi'(b_i - z_i)}{p''} = \frac{F'(z_i p''/p')}{p'}, \; i = 1,m$$

$$(x_1 + x_2 + \ldots + x_n) = (p'/p'')(z_1 + z_2 + \ldots + z_m).$$

These give the $m + n + 1$ equations from which the equilibrium price ratio, p'/p'', and the quantities x_1 to x_n and z_1 to z_m can be determined.

If the utility functions have the quadratic approximation formula, the supplies of good A from the various suppliers are, according to formula (7):

$$x_1 = \frac{\beta p'/p'' - (\alpha - 2\alpha_1 a_1)}{2(\alpha_1 + \beta_1(p'/p'')^2)}$$

and so on. Also the total for all n owners is:

$$x = \frac{n\beta p'/p'' - (\alpha - 2\alpha_1 a)}{2(\alpha_1 - \beta_1(p'/p'')^2)}.$$

The demands for good A, according to (13) are:

$$x_1 = \frac{\alpha - (\beta - 2\beta_1 b_1)\, p'/p''}{2(\alpha_1 - \beta_1 (p'/p'')^2)}.$$

and so on, that is a total of:

$$x'' = \frac{m\alpha - (m\beta - 2\beta_1 b)\, p'/p''}{2(\alpha_1 + \beta_1 (p'/p'')^2)}$$

From equating total supply and total demand, the equilibrium prices are:

$$\frac{p'}{p''} = \frac{(m+n)\alpha - 2\alpha_1 a}{(m+n)\beta - 2\beta_1 b}. \tag{28}$$

When introducing the numerical examples, the following equilibrium prices result: $m + n = 2$ at 0.500; $m + n = 3$ at 0.524; $m + n = 10$ at 0.548; $m + n = \infty$ at 0.555. One realizes that *the equilibrium prices depend on the number of persons who share in the possession of the goods, but not to a great extent.*

12. Exchange of Many Goods Among Many Persons

An arbitrary number, n, of persons may be in possession of different goods, the total number of these may be m. The utility function for each of the different goods may be assumed given and the total quantity of each of these available may be assumed known. Each proprietor will have *reached the maximum obtainable to him through exchange* and in proportion to the size of his initial level of property *if an equal priceworthiness exists for all goods in his possession*, because in the case of a lower priceworthiness existing for one of his goods, quantities of these goods would have to be disposed of to exchange some of the more valuable goods for them. From this condition, the price ratios of the various goods are derived, as well as the individual quantities usefully obtained by each owner of each of the goods.

If the utility function of the first good is F(x), their unit price is p', then the individual quantities which are held by n proprietors, are called x_1, x_2 to x_n and the total existing supply of these goods $a = x_1 + x_2 + \ldots x_n$; if in a similar pattern the utility function for the second good is $\Phi(y)$, the unit price is p'', then the individual quantities which are owned by the various proprietors are called y_1, y_2 to y_n and the total supply $b = y_1 + y_2 + \ldots y_n$, so that for the determination of the price ratio, p'/p'', the following n equations arise:

$$\frac{F'(x_i)}{p'} = \frac{\Phi'(y_i)}{p''}, \; i = 1,n.$$

By adding these equations one arrives, for the quadratic approximation of the utility function, at an expression for the price ratio p'/p'' similar to (28), with the distinction that in the former case the total number of exchanging persons was $n + m$, whereas here there are only n. The equation thus derived for the equilibrium prices is:

$$\frac{p'}{p''} = \frac{n\alpha - 2\alpha_1 a}{n\beta - 2\beta_1 b} \qquad (29)$$

which shows that *the price ratio of two goods remains unaffected by the exchange of any other goods* and develops in a way as if it took place in isolation between a given number of people. It must however be pointed out here that the price of certain goods remains dependent on the prices of all other goods in so far as it determines the number of persons able to participate in the possession of these goods, as will be proved in Chapter 14 in greater detail.

By equating the priceworthiness of the first and second goods, the second and third and so on, a total of $n(m - 1)$ equations are obtained, to which are added m equations of the form

$$x_1 + x_2 + \ldots + x_n = a$$
$$y_1 + y_2 + \ldots + y_n = b.$$

Finally the price of all exchanged goods must equal for each proprietor the gain from the quantity of goods parted with out of the initial stock, which supplies another n equations, through which the total number of equations comes to $nm + m$; these determine the equilibrium prices and the individual quantities of goods.

For a sample calculation three proprietors are assumed; of these A owns goods with a utility function of $x - x^2/1000$, with a quantity $a = 400$, B owns $b = 480$ with a utility function of $1.8y - y^2/800$, and C owns $c = 480$ with a utility function of $2z - z^2/600$. In accordance with (29) the equilibrium prices are as follows:

$$\frac{p'}{p''} = \frac{11}{12}, \frac{p'}{p'''} = \frac{1}{2}; \text{ and } \frac{p''}{p'''} = \frac{21}{22}$$

resulting in equilibrium price ratios of the three goods of $11 : 21 : 22$. After further application of the approach, not given here in detail because in Chapter 14 a simpler method will be explained, the individual quantities of the goods are found as follows:

$$
\begin{array}{llll}
\text{A has } x_1 = & 77, & y_1 = & 73, & z_1 = & 92 \\
\text{B has } x_2 = & 158, & y_2 = & 198, & z_2 = & 190 \\
\text{C has } x_3 = & 165, & y_3 = & 209, & z_3 = & 198 \\
& a = 400, & b = & 480, & c = & 480.
\end{array}
$$

After the exchange of goods has taken place in this manner, A, whose initial utility was 240, has reached 366, which means a gain of 126, proprietor B went from 576 to 760, indicating a gain of 184, and owner C was able to go from 576 to 790, indicating a gain of 214. The result of this calculation is that the earlier established fact, that in an exchange at equilibrium prices two owners obtain equal profit, does not apply any longer in the case of an exchange between several proprietors, but that *in an exchange at equilibrium prices between several proprietors the richer obtains the greatest gain, but in proportion to the initial possession the poorer proprietor has obtained the highest percentage gain.*

If we note that when only proprietors A and B exchanged their goods at equilibrium prices, their gain amounted to 93, then the important conclusion follows that *the gain obtainable through exchange will be the greater, the greater the number of goods which are obtainable by way of exchange.*

Not only the individual quantities of goods but also the number of different goods are dependent on the size of the original endowment. The poor owner cannot obtain expensive goods through exchange; this will be discussed in detail in Chapter 14. The individual proprietor cannot exchange an arbitrary number of different goods for his initial possessions, but remains confined to the exchange of such goods whose priceworthiness corresponds to his level of property. Before this is further explained the remarkable fact should be noted that in exchanging more than two goods between more than two owners, *the new formation of the property level in accordance with the equilibrium prices between the original owners of goods can no longer be carried out through immediate exchange, but makes intermediate transactions necessary.*

According to the example, proprietor A must buy a quantity $z_1 = 92$ of goods C at a price ratio of 1:2 so that he would have to pay 184 units of his goods C for it. As C can make use of the goods of A only in the manner $x_3 = 165$, A can receive at this stage of only half of $165 = 82.5$ units of C's goods. With B, A wishes to exchange $y_1 = 73$ units at a price ratio of 11/21 so that he would have to give $(21/11)73 = 139.5$ units of his goods for them. But proprietor B does not wish to have 139.5 of A, but instead $x_2 = 158$. It can therefore be seen that *the exchange cannot take place between the original owners of the goods; in addition to the exchange an intermediate transaction will have to take place.*

Proprietor A could obtain the property level desired by him by way of the following exchange transactions:

1. A parts with 165 units of his goods A for 82.5 units of goods C.
2. A parts with 158 units of his goods for $(11/21)158 = 83$ units of goods B. This way A has taken 10 units of goods B into storage as he required only 73.
3. B, whose demand for goods A is satisfied, desires to obtain 190 units of goods C for which he will have to part with $(22/21)190 = 199$ units of his possession. Thus B has reached the level of possession he desired.
4. A who had taken on 10 units of goods B in excess of his requirement, but who however could not satisfy his demand for goods C in the first exchange and received 9.5 units too few, is now in a position to offer to owner C those ten units of goods B taken into storage which owner C requires, at a price-in-balance ratio of 21/22 for 9.5 units of goods C.

In this way distribution has been carried out in *four* transactions in accordance with equilibrium prices, that is by balancing demand and supply, which would have been possible in *three* exchange transactions if each proprietor could have obtained the desired goods directly from their original owner.

With the increase in the number of persons involved in the exchanges and the number of goods to be exchanged – as can be observed in the sample calculation – the number of exchange transactions which take place not for the purpose of consumption but for the purpose of trading will also increase, that is to enable the trader to carry out other desired exchange transactions. Of necessity the *economic profession of the merchant* evolves out of the transactions not intended to promote lasting possession of the goods traded. However, in spite of the appearance of the merchant the exchange of goods remains a cumbersome activity until *money* is introduced into trade. With money the number of exchanges is reduced because the possibility is created to obtain with a single transaction the most favourable quantity of any goods according to the level of one's possession. If it now becomes theoretically possible through the introduction of money to obtain the desired quantity directly from the original owner of the goods, and thereby the just-described economic reasoning for the appearance of the merchant becomes invalid, there is nevertheless no argument about the fact that in practical economic life the activities of the merchant are indispensable for the formation of prices.

13. Exchange for Money, or Purchase and Sale

The price ratio of various goods is derived from the provision that for every individual owner the priceworthiness for all the various goods in his possession must be equal. If the unit price for a given variety of goods is taken as a price unit, be it for a hectolitre of wheat or a hundredweight of coal, a kilo of gold etc., then the prices of all other varieties of goods evolve, expressed in this unit. The goods whose price is taken as the unit for the determination of prices for all remaining goods, is called *money*, while in contrast to money all other goods are called merchandise. The exchange of merchandise for money is called *purchase* or *sale*; the merchandise is *paid for* with money.

There is no need for an argument to prove that for use as money such merchandise is best suited which is not prone to wear, slow disintegration or breakage in accidents, which in spite of little weight and small size possesses great value, meaning it must be rare, which can be infinitely divided and in its total mass cannot be enlarged without difficulty or reduced through consumption. It is therefore no coincidence that the precious metals, which fulfil these demands more satisfactorily than any other goods, were introduced as currency.

The goods which play the role of money win through this an essential characteristic distinguishing them from all other goods. Money, which does not serve direct consumption or pleasure which makes it independent of the owner's appreciation of it as a source of pleasure, *retains always a value proportional to its quantity*. Its utility graph is therefore a straight line and the utility y, of a quantity, x, is expressed in the simple equation:

$$y = px.$$

Even if one is not tempted to accept this formula in its full severity, it will nevertheless have to be recognized in the circumstances of practical economic life as undoubtedly to the point.

By the introduction of money the determination of the prices of goods is derived whose quantity is a and whose utility function is $F(x)$ simply because of the condition that $F(a-x) + px$ must become a maximum; that is:

$$p = F'(a-x);$$

that means that *the price of a good must be equal to its marginal utility.* For the utility function $F(x) = \alpha x - \alpha_1 x^2$,

$$p = \alpha - 2\alpha_1(a-x)$$

so that at a price of p and a possession of goods a_1 supplies are:

$$x = a_1 - (\alpha - p)/2\alpha_1.$$

If a number of n_1 owners of the merchandise exist who together possess the quantity of goods, a, their joint total supplies are:

$$x = \{a - n_1(\alpha - p)\}/2\alpha_1.$$

For the purchaser who bought a quantity x of goods at the price p, utility is $\alpha x - \alpha_1 x^2 - px$ which becomes a maximum when:

$$x = (\alpha - p)/2\alpha_1.$$

This leads, with a number n'' of buyers, to a total demand of:

$$x = n''(\alpha - p)/2\alpha_1.$$

By balancing the total demand with the total supply, one arrives at the equilibrium price when the total number of possible owners, the sum of buyers and sellers $n' + n''$, is n, of

$$p = \alpha - 2\alpha_1\, a/n; \tag{30}$$

this means, *the equilibrium price of a good equals the marginal utility which it would have if its total supply were equally distributed among all who are in a position to participate in its ownership.* The answer to the question: which 'economic persons' can participate in the ownership of a given merchandise, will follow in Chapter 14.

14. Balance of the Budget

The first condition for a balanced budget was discussed in Chapter 12. *The priceworthiness of all goods for consumption must be equal.* If the various goods have utility functions F(x), Φ(y), ψ(z) etc. and in order the unit prices of p', p'', p''' etc., the priceworthiness for all will have to be the same:

$$w = \frac{F'(x)}{p'} = \frac{\Phi'(y)}{p''} = \frac{\Phi'(z)}{p'''}. \tag{31}$$

The sums of all amounts paid for the individual goods must equal the income, e, of the consumer; it follows that:

$$e = p'x + p''y + p'''z + \ldots.$$

or, in consideration of the priceworthiness expressed in (31):

$$ew = xF'(x) + y\Phi'(y) + z\psi'(z) + \ldots$$

The income, e, multiplied by the achievable priceworthiness, w, of the goods represents a measure of the economic importance of the consumer, which can be expressed also as his *buying power*. At a given income the buying power grows in a direct ratio to the price-worthiness at which goods can be obtained. The priceworthiness increases, the smaller the quantity of the individual goods and the larger the number of the categories of goods available for consumption. The limit of the expansion of consumption to as large a number of different goods as possible is reached when no further goods can be purchased at an equal priceworthiness to that achieved for the bulk of possessions, i.e. when all varieties of consumption goods not yet obtained have a lower priceworthiness, that is are more expensive, than the goods representing the 'bulk of possessions'. Therefore the second condition to be added to the first for the balance of the budget is: *Consumption must be extended over as large a number of*

different goods as possible so that only such goods are excluded from
consumption which are more expensive than those corresponding to the
achievable priceworthiness given a certain income.

For further clarification, suppose for example that the utility
function of the cheapest consumer good is $\alpha x - \alpha_1 x^2$, so that at a
unit price, p, the first unit of the merchandise which has a value α per
unit of money, supplies a consumption value of α/p which is larger
than would be possible with the purchase and use of any other good.
If then, starting with the cheapest good and moving towards the
more expensive, the utility functions of the goods are $\beta y - \beta_1 y^2$,
$\gamma z - \gamma_1 z^2$ and so on, then according to the rule of equal priceworthiness, quantities must be obtained such that:

$$\frac{\alpha - 2\alpha_1 x}{p'} = \frac{\beta - 2\beta_1 y}{p''} = \frac{\gamma - 2\gamma_1 z}{p'''} = \ldots = w$$

that is, the amounts spent on the purchase of the various goods
come to:

$$p'x = p'(\alpha - wp')/2\alpha_1$$

$$p''y = p''(\beta - wp'')/2\beta_1$$

$$p'''z = p'''(\gamma - wp''')/2\gamma_1$$

and so on. By adding up these individual amounts which must
together equal income, e, the achievable priceworthiness is arrived at
as follows:

$$w = \frac{\left(\frac{\alpha}{2\alpha_1} p' + \frac{\beta}{2\beta_1} p'' + \frac{\gamma}{2\gamma_1} p''' + \ldots\right) - e}{\frac{p'^2}{2\alpha_1} + \frac{p''^2}{2\beta_1} + \frac{p'''^2}{2\gamma_1}} \tag{32}$$

The larger the number of goods included in the purchase the
larger w will become. As the purchaser moves to more expensive
goods, a good will be reached, say with unit price of p^n and utility
function $\lambda u - \lambda_1 u^2$, for which the priceworthiness of its first unit
purchased equals λ/p^n of the priceworthiness w. The ratio $\alpha/2\alpha_1$

denotes the quantity of the first good for which the consumption reaches its maximum, for which saturation is reached. It follows that the amount of money with which saturation can be achieved is $p'\alpha/2\alpha_1$. Describing the sum as s, for which total saturation can be achieved for all goods purchased, the condition for the balance of the budget can be expressed as:

$$w = \frac{s-e}{\dfrac{p'^2}{2\alpha_1} + \dfrac{p''^2}{2\beta_1} + \ldots}. \tag{33}$$

If the following values are set for the three cheapest goods at $\alpha = 1$, $\alpha_1 = 1/1000$, $p' = 11$, $\gamma = 2$, $\gamma_1 = 1/600$, $p''' = 22$, $\beta = 1.8$, $\beta_1 = 1/800$, $p'' = 21$, then a priceworthiness of $w = (33820 - e)/382100$ is obtained. For an income of $e = 4400$ a priceworthiness of $w = 0.077$ would be achievable. Purchases would extend to all goods available at a priceworthiness greater than 0.077. If a fourth good had the utility function of $2.1u - u^2/1200$ and the price of $p^4 = 25$, so that its first unit had a priceworthiness of $2.1/25 = 0.084$, then the overall priceworthiness would, after inclusion of this good, amount to $w = (65320 - e)/757100$, which means that for $e = 4400$, $w = 0.0805$.

If the fifth next cheapest good had, at a price of $p^s = 20$, a utility function of $1.6 v - v^2/600$, so that its first unit had a priceworthiness of $1.6/20 = 0.08$, this would, at an income of 4400, be too expensive. The income would have to grow above 4752, at which the four cheapest goods could be purchased at a priceworthiness of 0.08, if the fifth good is to be included in consumption.

For the owner of an income of 4400 who can purchase at a priceworthiness of 0.0805, the quantities of goods $x = 57$, $y = 44$, $z = 69$ and $u = 53$ are derived from the following equations:

$$w = (\alpha - 2\alpha_1 x)/p' = (\beta - 2\beta_1 y)/p'' = \ldots.$$

When choosing goods for a household, those which satisfy the same needs must not be purchased simultaneously as every need can be satisfied only once at a certain time. If for instance the need for fuel is satisfied by the purchase of peat, it cannot be looked after at the same time through the purchase of firewood or coal; the same applies to food, light sources, clothes etc. It is apparent that in trying to find a balance in the budgeting for such goods which satisfy the same needs, these must be considered as one group.

It will be simplest to demonstrate by way of an example how within such a group the constellation of ratios of quantities of goods to one another has to be established. If the utility function for potatoes for x kilograms is $x - x^2/10$, at a price of $p' = 6$ pfennigs per kilogram, the utility function for bread for y kilograms is $2y - y^2/3$, at a price of $p'' = 15$ pfennigs per kilogram, then the fullest enjoyment of potatoes, that is full satisfaction, would be reached at a consumption of 5 kg, in contrast for bread at a consumption of 3 kg. The 5 kg potatoes cost 30 pfennigs, for 3 kg bread the cost is 45 pfennigs. If the higher price for bread is to be justified then it must offer, apart from eliminating hunger, some other advantages such as better taste, easier digestibility etc. As 1.75 kg potatoes offer the same nourishment as 1 kg bread, the total overview of the matter will be made easier when the value equation of the potatoes is converted to measuring units of $1\frac{2}{3}$ kg of which each will then cost 10 pfennigs. The conversion results in $1\frac{2}{3}y - \frac{1}{10}(1\frac{2}{3}y)^2 = 1\frac{2}{3}y - \frac{5}{18}y^2$. Accordingly the utility function of bread shows for units of equal value of nourishment in comparison to potatoes, a surplus of $2y - \frac{1}{3}y^2 - (1\frac{2}{3} - \frac{5}{18}y^2) = \frac{1}{3} - \frac{1}{18}y^2$. This surplus in utility is due to the advantages of the bread, i.e. the better taste or the greater digestibility for which the price of $15 - 10 = 5$ pfennigs has to be paid.

The priceworthiness at which the surplus value of the bread's better taste and digestibility is obtained must equal the priceworthiness which corresponds to the balance of the budget. If the priceworthiness is 0.05, then, for bread and potatoes as mere foodstuffs, the equation $\frac{1}{10}(1\frac{2}{3} - \frac{5}{9}y) = 0.05$ would have to be fulfilled, from which $y = 2.1$. The advantages of the bread, however, demand instead the fulfilling of $\frac{1}{5}(\frac{1}{3} - \frac{1}{9}y') = 0.05$, from which results $y' = 0.75$. Therefore 0.75 kg bread must be purchased, of the total quantity of bread-and-potatoes 2.1 units, i.e. $2.1 - 0.75 = 1.35$ measuring units of potatoes, or as the measuring unit of potatoes was $= 1.66$ kg, $= (1\frac{2}{3})(1.35) = 2.25$ kg potatoes.

There is room for a second example. For cigars made of Brazilian tobacco which are sold at a price of 5 pfennigs each, the utility function may be, for an annual consumption of x cigars, $x - x^2/4800$, so that a smoker with an annual consumption of 2400 cigars reaches the highest measure of pleasure obtainable from the cigars at 1200. The smoking needs may however be satisfied by Havana cigars each of which is priced at 50 pfennigs in accordance with the utility function $1.5y - (3/6400) y^2$ so that initially, by way of a consumption of 1600 cigars, the same pleasure of 1200 can be achieved as by way of using 2400 Brazilian cigars. If one dealt merely with satisfying the average smoking needs, one would pay 1.5 times the price of the Brazilian cigars for the Havana cigars, that is, 7.5 pfennigs each. The increase price of $50 - 7.5 = 42.5$ pfennigs is justified by the pleasure which the Havana cigars offer by way of their fine aroma and taste, which may be estimated at $3y - y^2/1280$. The total pleasure of the Havana cigars is therefore:

$$1.5\,y - \frac{3y^2}{6400} + 3y - \frac{y^2}{1280} = 4.5y - \frac{y^2}{800}.$$

Someone who can satisfy his needs at a priceworthiness of 0.05, will smoke a quantity of x' of the Brazilian cigars from $(1 - x'/2400)/5 = 0.05$, giving $x' = 1800$. In accordance with the surplus value of the Havana cigars, for which must be paid 42.5 pfennigs each, consumption is a quantity y', which derives from $(3 - y'/640)/42.5 = 0.05$, giving $y' = 560$. As the normal smoking needs are satisfied as much by 560 Havana cigars as by $(1.5)(560) = 840$ Brazilian cigars there will be, apart from the Havana, $1800 - 840 = 960$ Brazilian cigars available for smoking.

If however the smoker, in accordance with his income, can purchase only up to a priceworthiness of 0.0706, $y' = 0$; he could not afford to smoke Havana cigars. But if the smoker is well enough off to be able to satisfy his needs even at a priceworthiness of 0.0167, he could afford to smoke nothing but Havana cigars because for these the figure $y' = 1467$ arises, through which $(1.5)(1467) = 2200$ Brazilian cigars are arrived at which may be smoked at a priceworthiness of 0.0167.

After looking at these examples the third condition for the determination of the balance in the budget becomes apparent. The goods must be sorted into groups which fulfil equal value demands, that is they serve the same needs. Within each group the various goods will appear as units which satisfy equally and with the same price for these units. From the excess of the prices of individual goods above the common price of the group and from the excess shown in the utility function of the individual goods above the common utility function of the group, derive at a given common priceworthiness of the total holdings the quantities of the individual goods.

When applying the rules established for the balance in the budget, the highest achievable degree of pleasure at a given level of income is determined. No goods which form the proper basis of the state of balance in the budget can be exchanged at the existing prices for any of the other goods without a decrease in the level of pleasure.

As the estimation of the value of the goods depends largely on personal assessment, understandably ten people who can dispose of the same level of income will, in the effort to balance the budget, arrive at different results, even disregarding the fact that one cannot speak here of a strictly arithmetic procedure anyway. Only in special cases where values which are free of personal assessment form the basis, can the rules develop for the balance in the budget to be arithmetically applied. One could for example assume that a colonel has at his disposal a certain sum for the upkeep of the horses in his regiment; assuming that no lack of the necessary experience exists, it can very well be estimated how much of the total amount has to be spent on straw, oats, hay, horseshoeing etc.

Finally it should be remembered that the achievement of a balance in the budget is impossible with a scant income. If the poor person wants to distribute his means over the full range of goods within his buying power so that equal priceworthiness is obtained, only extremely small quantities of each merchandise can be purchased, which can easily result in a situation in which food cannot be obtained in sufficient quantities to sustain life. The fulfilment of the need for other items like clothing, shelter, fuel etc. can be regulated in accordance with the rules established for a balance in the budget, but nourishment cannot, understandably, go below a certain minimum quantity. Only after securing basic existence can the achievement of a balance in the budget for other items be contemplated. Reaching the highest measure of utility in the application of one's income which is supported by a balance in the budget, which in turn is tied to the inhibiting issue of eking out a bare existence, leads, with a minimal income, to the situation of not an absolute maximum of utility, but only of a maximum relative to the inhibiting factor.

According to the given situation there exists for every person in possession of an income the desire to obtain a certain quantity of certain goods. From the sum of individual demand derives the total demand which is therefore dependent on the total number of 'economic' persons – i.e. persons able to dispose of an income – on the extent or size of their incomes, on the price of the specific merchandise, but also on the prices of all other goods, because price-worthiness is derived from these prices at which each individual person carries out his or her purchases.

15. The Formation of Capital

In the investigations of the balanced budget it was supposed that the income obtained over a certain period of time was consumed over the same period. The question should be posed whether it would not perhaps be useful to put away part of the income as savings to be consumed in the future, which means a reduction of pleasure for the present to ensure a greater pleasure in the future.

To begin with, let us assume that the annual income, e, is ensured at an unalterable level. It may further be assumed that the savings as capital can earn an interest rate of i. If an amount, x, is saved of the income, e, the income usable at present comes to e − x while for the future an income of e + ix is ensured. However, a pleasure which can be anticipated in the future is, as pointed out in Chapter 2, appreciated less than an equal pleasure available in the present. According to the personal view of the consumer, the degree of reduction in the value is estimated as more or less considerable. The easy-going person or even the careless will attach far less value to the pleasures of the future than to those of the present, compared to the careful, thoughtful or timid person.

If the pleasure G of the following year is estimated at $G/(1 + i_0)$ and that of the year after at $G/(1 + i_0)^2$, whereby i_0 is the interest rate which the person asks, then the continuous annual pleasure G has the present value of:

$$\Sigma\left(\frac{1}{1 + i_0} + \frac{1}{(1 + i_0)^2} + \ldots\right)G$$

which in total is G/i_0.

If the price of consumer goods with a utility function of F(a) is p, then with savings, x, of income, e, present pleasure is $F((e-x)/p)$ while in the future a pleasure of $F((e + ix)/p)$ will occur annually. The present value of present and future consumption is therefore:

$$S = F\left(\frac{e-x}{p}\right) + \frac{1}{i_0}F\left(\frac{e+ix}{p}\right).$$

The value of x at which this sum of pleasure becomes a maximum can be obtained by differentiating with respect to x and setting the differential quotient to zero. This will deliver the condition:

$$\frac{F'((e-x)/p)}{F'((e+ix)/p)} = \frac{i}{i_0}. \tag{34}$$

This is the *basic equation for the formation of capital* which can be expressed in the following words: *The marginal utility of the pleasure remaining for the present after putting away savings for the future must relate to the utility of the pleasure which is increased by interest, as does the offered interest to the demanded interest.* If the offered interest is no higher than the demanded interest, x must equal zero; the incentive to save disappears. Once again the situation may be clarified by adopting a definite form for the utility function. If $F(a) = \alpha a - \alpha_1 a^2$, then it follows that the basic equation for the formation of capital is:

$$\frac{-\alpha + 2\alpha_1\{(e-x)/p\}}{\alpha i - 2\alpha_1^2 i\{(e+ix)/p\}} = \frac{i}{i_0}$$

which results in:

$$x = \frac{p}{2\alpha_1}\left(\alpha - 2\alpha_1\frac{e}{p}\right)\frac{i-i_0}{i^2+i_0}.$$

As the priceworthiness, w, at which the goods could be obtained without savings is $(\alpha - 2\alpha_1 e/p)/p$, then:

$$x = \frac{p^2}{2\alpha_1} w \frac{i-i_0}{i^2+i_0}. \tag{35}$$

If income can be stretched over the purchase of a number of different goods, then savings would have to be made when purchasing the other goods in a similar manner which would be:

$$y = \frac{p''^2}{2\beta_1} w \frac{i-i_0}{i^2+i_0}$$

and soon. Hence the total capital $k = x + y + \ldots$ saved in a similar manner for all goods is:

$$k = \Sigma \left(\frac{p'^2}{2\alpha_1} + \frac{p''^2}{2\beta_1} + \ldots \right) w \frac{i - i_0}{i^2 + i_0}.$$

According to Chapter 14, if s denotes the amount of money for which for all purchased goods total saturation would be reached, this can instead be expressed:

$$k = (s - e) \frac{i - i_0}{i^2 + i_0} \tag{36}$$

It can be recognized from this equation that savings should be the larger, the more the income falls short of the amount which would afford total satisfaction. This can be explained because the more unsatisfactory the present remains, the stronger is the effort to change things for the better, at least for the future. One should not however allow oneself to draw the seriously erroneous conclusion that the poorer should now save more ardently than the richer. If the income, e, is minimal, then the number of pleasurable goods which can be included in the consumption will be smaller and only the cheapest goods can be purchased, so that with the shrinking of e, s will also be reduced and the difference, $s - e$, will decrease considerably faster than e. Finally it has to be observed, following on from the remarks made at the end of Chapter 14, that from that amount of income which is spent on the maintenance of bare existence no savings at all can be made.

It should not remain unmentioned that savings which increase by the offered interest rate i nevertheless reach a maximum. This interest rate is found, when one differentiates with respect to i, at:

$$i = i_0 + (i_0^2 + i_0)^{0.5}.$$

For instance, at $i_0 = 0.03$, $i = 0.21$. This initially surprising situation is nevertheless easily explained when it is remembered that with a high interest rate even moderate savings will supply a considerable gain for the future. The interest rate at which the incentive to save begins to diminish is however so high that this result is without any practical implications.

The priceworthiness which amounts, without saving, to $w = \{\alpha - 2\alpha_1(e/p)\}/p$, will become, due to savings of x:

$$w' = \{\alpha - 2\alpha_1(e - x)/p\}/p$$

which will, by substituting for x, become:

$$w' = \frac{\alpha - 2\alpha_1(e/p)}{p}\left(\frac{i^2 + i}{i^2 + i_0}\right)$$

$$= w(i^2 + i)/(i^2 + i_0).$$

The pleasure of the future has the present value of:

$$\frac{1}{i_0}\left[\alpha\frac{e + ix}{p} - \alpha_1\left(\frac{e + ix}{p}\right)^2\right]$$

that is, a priceworthiness of

$$\frac{1}{i_0 p}\left[\alpha - 2\alpha_1\left(\frac{e + ix}{p}\right)\right]$$

from this, after substituting the value of x from (35), the same priceworthiness, (37), results as for the pleasure of the present.

The basic rule applying to the formation of capital could therefore also be expressed as follows: *The savings must be made large enough so that the priceworthiness of the present value of total future pleasure equals the priceworthiness of the pleasure remaining for the present.*

The calculation by which the most useful extent of saving for the present is worked out will have to be repeated in the following year for the income increased by the interest of the already-saved capital. But the most useful extent of saving in the second year will be a little smaller than that of the first year, namely:

$$k' = (s - e - ix)(i - i_0)/(i^2 + i_0)$$

that is, smaller by $ix(i - i_0)/(i^2 + i_0)$. Only after a number of years will the interest of the slowly saved capital have grown to such an extent that it exceeds the amount of the new savings, so that the real consumption reaches the size of the permanently ensured income e, which could have been utilized annually without any saving. As the results of such an economically correctly executed savings scheme can be reaped only in the distant future, depending on the interest rate in about twelve to twenty years, not everyone will be inclined to base their calculation on the presupposition of an indefinite period of pleasure. The more the period of pleasure on which the calculation is based will be shortened, the smaller the incentive for saving will become.

If it now appears, as in the earlier-mentioned case, where the offered interest rate is equal to the demanded interest rate, that to make no savings is useful, then even when the offered interest rate lies below the demanded one, a loan or, what amounts to the same thing, the using up of part of the capital for the purpose of increasing current utility is recommended. The increase in utility in the present amounts to the same as does the present value of the loss for the future. Nevertheless, it can occur that even in the case where the offered interest rate is lower than that demanded, instead of a decrease of capital, savings are made.

All investigations so far into the most useful level of saving were based on the assumption of a constant income assured for all future. It must here be stressed that an essential incentive for the putting away of savings lies in the provision made for the future to insure against possible future reductions in income, following the justifiable exhortation: 'Save so you will be provided for in times of need.' How to calculate in such cases may be demonstrated in a simple example. If it is assumed that income, e, will be reduced from next year by v, then by maintaining, for example, the adherence to the basic utility function, the sum of the present and future utility at a capital saving x would be obtained at:

$$S = \alpha\left(\frac{e - x}{p}\right) - \alpha_1\left(\frac{e - x}{p}\right)^2 + \frac{i}{i_0}\left[\alpha\left(\frac{e - v + ix}{p}\right)\right.$$
$$\left. - \alpha_1\left(\frac{e - v + ix}{p}\right)^2\right].$$

This sum reaches its highest value for:

$$x = \frac{p}{2\alpha_1}\left(\alpha - 2\alpha_1 \frac{e}{p}\right)\frac{i - i_0}{i^2 + i_0} + v\frac{i}{i^2 + i_0}. \tag{38}$$

Savings will have to be made even if the demanded interest rate i_0

is higher than the offered interest rate i, in consideration of the coming loss v of income. A careful economist will estimate his savings in accordance with the likely losses which therefore are to be interpreted as insurance premiums against possible losses. From this point of view, the accumulation of a 'treasure' without any interest, as it can occur in an economically undeveloped situation, can appear to be justifiable.

Finally, it hardly needs mentioning that the method of determining savings in accordance with these rules will not easily be put into practice. The calculation would have to be based on a personal estimate of the utility function and of the demanded interest rate; it is therefore necessary to maintain the absolutely unavoidable method of estimating, even up to the finalization of the extent of the necessary savings. The evolved rules have to be followed here, if subconsciously, if the final result is to be the right one. It may be doubted whether the discovery of the rules developed for the formation of capital can be utilized for the enlightenment of the dark and unsafe path of estimating matters. From the scientific point of view, the establishing of these laws maintains their importance and unimpeded value, just as the research into currents and movements of the atmosphere does not lose its scientific value if its predictions cannot always be used to forecast the weather.

16. Exchange Impeded by Commercial Costs

As a rule, trading of goods cannot take place without costs, which is where expenditure for packaging, freight, storage, customs duties, loss of interest payments, insurance, overheads for agents, advertising, profit margins for merchants etc. belong; these are to be summed up as 'commercial costs'. The gain obtainable through the exchange of goods usually suffers considerable reduction due to these trading expenses.

The owner of a supply of merchandise a, with utility function $F(a)$, reaches, after the sale of a quantity, x, at a unit price of p, a utility level of:

$$F(a - x) + px$$

which will reach a maximum at

$$p = -F'(a - x).$$

If unavoidable trading expenses, u, and the merchant's profit margin, g, are added to the unit price, then the buyer will have to pay $p + u + g$ for the unit in order to obtain a quantity x. The buyer's utility is, after the purchase:

$$F(x) - (p + u + g)x$$

which becomes a maximum at:

$$F'(x) = p + u + g.$$

After introducing the formula $F(x) = \alpha x - \alpha_1 x^2$ the seller's offer will be:

$$x' = \{p - (\alpha - 2\alpha_1 a)\}/2\alpha_1$$

and the buyer's demand:

$$x'' = (\alpha - p - u - g)/2\alpha_1,$$

deriving from this the balancing of supply and demand at a price obtained by the seller:

$$p = \alpha - \alpha_1 a - (u + g)/2 \tag{39}$$

and the price faced by the buyer of:

$$p + u + g = \alpha - \alpha_1 a + (u + g)/2. \tag{40}$$

Equations (39) and (40) show that *both the seller and the buyer have to bear half each of the trading costs and the profit*. The quantity of goods traded is:

$$x = (2\alpha_1 a - u - g)/4\alpha_1 \tag{41}$$

which demonstrates the extent to which *the turnover of goods is reduced, due to trading expenses and the trading profit*.

The total profit of seller, buyer and merchant, that is, the total economic gain in the trading transaction, is:

$$\begin{aligned} G &= \alpha\,(a - x) - \alpha_1\,(a - x)^2 - \alpha a + \alpha_1 a^2 + px + \\ &\quad \alpha x - \alpha_1 x^2 - (p + u + g)x + gx \\ &= 2\alpha_1 a x - 2\alpha_1 x^2 - ux \end{aligned}$$

or by introducing the traded quantity x given in (41):

$$G = [(2\alpha_1 a - u)^2 - g^2]/8\alpha_1. \tag{42}$$

The economic gain from the turnover of goods is therefore the smaller, the bigger the profit margin added by the merchant. The widely held opinion, that the damage done to the producer and the consumer of the goods by the profit margin added by the merchant will be balanced overall economically by his gain, is therefore proven wrong. The harm caused in economic terms by the addition of the profit margin of the merchant is explained by the reduced turnover of goods.

According to (41) the commercial gain, gx, which, after substituting for x, is:

$$G' = (2\alpha_1 a - u - g)g/4\alpha_1$$

reaches a maximum at

$$g = (2\alpha_1 a - u)/2$$

for which:

$$G' = (2\alpha_1 a - u)^2/16\alpha_1 \tag{43}$$

while the economic gain, at this most favourable profit rate for the trader, amounts to:

$$G'' = 3(2\alpha_1 a - u)^2/32\alpha_1. \tag{44}$$

In a case where the merchant is in a position to fix his profit margin at a level most favourable to him, he will draw two-thirds of the total economic gain achievable in the exchange of goods or double the amount that the producer and the consumer gain together. However, due to competition the trader will be able only in exceptional cases to fix the profit margin at a level most favourable to him. Equations (42) and (43) show that it is more profitable for the merchant, as for all others taking part in the transfer of goods, to reduce his trading expenses u to as low a level as possible. If for convenience the ratio $(2\alpha_1 a - u)^2/\alpha_1 = D$ is introduced, then the economic gain in the trading of goods, in a case where the merchant adds the profit margin most favourable to him, results from (44) in 3D/32. If the producer of the goods could have sold directly to the consumer, then, from (42) with $g = 0$, an economic gain of D/8 would be obtained which would be shared equally by the seller and the buyer. In the extreme case therefore, due to the mediation of the merchant, one-quarter of the obtainable economic gain of D/8 in the trading transaction is lost as the total profit is reduced to 3D/32.

Calculations demonstrate that *as far as possible the mediation of the merchant in the transfer of goods must be avoided and the direct sale by a producer of a merchandise to the consumer must be striven after*. This goal gains important when it is remembered that in the majority of cases goods pass from the producer to the consumer not only through the hands of one merchant but through a series of traders, each of whom adds a profit margin. On the other hand, we must not lose sight of the fact that the merchant can exploit his business as a monopoly only in exceptional situations. But in most circumstances, under the pressure of free competition, he is not in a position to apply the profit margin most favourable to him and has to be satisfied with a moderate profit. The trader is – this barely needs to be stressed – nevertheless indispensable in economic activity in most instances and contributes with his knowledge of sources of supplies and markets for goods. It is in the trade with foreign and overseas countries that the merchant gains his decisive economic importance.

If the receipt of goods from abroad or the dispatch of merchandise to other countries were carried out directly between the producer and the consumer, then the national economy would gain $D/16$ in the turnover of goods. If the transfer were negotiated by a local trader, then he could, when applying the most favourable profit margin, gain for himself a profit of $D/16$, while the producer or consumer of the merchandise at home would still be left with a gain of $D/64$ so that the total profit for the home economy would amount to $5D/64$, an increase compared to a situation without the participation of a trader. If the negotiations are, however, carried out by a foreign trader, then the profit for the home economy would be confined to $D/64$. This simple calculation demonstrates *the extraordinary importance of the local trader who engages in import or export trade.* It is of the greatest importance for the home economy to have local merchants negotiate the trade with foreign and overseas countries. The full benefit for the home community only ensues if the trader in the home country is directly in touch with the foreign producers or consumers, for example through branch offices abroad whose profits are returned to the home country. In further exposition this explains *the great advantages in having colonies and shipping lines run from the mother country.*

17. Customs Duty

Among the incidental expenses which add to the problems of turning over goods, customs duty is of exceptional significance to the national economy.

Goods with a utility function $\alpha x - \alpha_1 x^2$ and unit price, p, represent to someone who buys x an increase in the utility of his holdings of $\alpha x - \alpha_1 x^2 - px$, with a maximum for $x = (\alpha - p)/2\alpha_1$, when:

$$G = (\alpha - p)^2/4\alpha_1.$$

For n persons who purchase the good, total demand is $n(\alpha - p)/2\alpha_1$ and the increase in utility amounts to:

$$G = n(\alpha - p)^2/4\alpha_1.$$

If the price of the good were determined by imports from another country, then the price would rise due to customs duty, z, but the demand and, following that, the imported quantity decrease. The overseas producers of the good, in order to regain at least partially the lost market, will reduce the price of the goods as much as possible. The price will therefore not reach the level of $p + z$, but, according to the drop in price of r originated by the overseas producers, turn into $p + z - r$. After the introduction of the customs duty the demand will become $n(\alpha - p - z + r)/2\alpha_1$ and the gain in utility obtained by the consumers of the good at home will be:

$$G' = n(\alpha - p - z + r)^2/4\alpha_1.$$

They suffer a loss of $G'' = G - G'$ which is:

$$G'' = n[2(\alpha - p)(z - r) - (z - r)^2]/4\alpha_1.$$

If the home country can supply the quantity necessary to satisfy the total demand, then the import, after being charged with customs duty, remains $n(\alpha - p - z + r)/2\alpha_1 - a$, and the profit from customs duty amounts to:

$$Z = n(\alpha - p - z + r)z/2\alpha_1 - az.$$

The producers of the good in the home country who, prior to the introduction of the customs duty, received a price of p will now be able to sell their supplies, a, at a unit price of $p + z - r$, thereby gaining:

$$G''' = a(z - r).$$

If the takings Z from customs duty are added to this gain and the loss to the consumers of the goods at home are deducted, then the remaining economic usefulness of the customs duty is:

$$N = n\{(\alpha - 2\alpha_1 a/n - p)2r + r^2 - z^2\}/4\alpha_1. \tag{45}$$

This is the basic equation for the assessment of matters in regard to customs duties.

In all cases where a reduction in the price of goods to be paid to foreign countries cannot be expected, the introduction of customs duties is in terms of the national economy disadvantageous, because the gain N from $r = 0$ becomes negative. The disadvantage grows in a quadratic ratio to the rate of customs duty. If the home economy is to remain at least unaffected by the introduction of a customs duty rate of z, then the reduction in price r must at least reach a level which is obtained using (45) by setting it to zero:

$$r = -(\alpha - 2\alpha_1 a/n - p) + \{z^2 + (\alpha - 2\alpha_1 a/n - p)^2\}^{0.5}.$$

If imports did not take place so that consumption had to be restricted to the goods, a, produced locally, then the price for the goods would come to $p' = \alpha - 2\alpha_1 a/n$. If p' is substituted into the formula for r, then:

$$(p' - p + r)^2 + = z^2 + (p' - p)^2. \tag{46}$$

Here $p' - p$ is the increase of the local price arrived at without import of foreign goods, lying above the price of the foreign goods

Figure 5

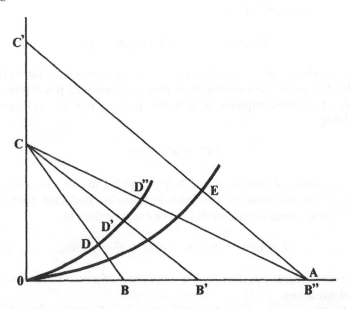

at the level it was prior to the introduction of customs duty, while $p' - p + r$ demonstrates this difference after the introduction of customs duty.

The condition given in (46) is easily demonstrated graphically. If, in Figure 5, the line OC directed at a right angle to OA equals $p' - p$ and with CO out of C a circle $ODD'D''$ is drawn and, in the direction of O to A introduces the level of the rate of customs duty z, equalling OB, then the price reduction r following this rate of customs duty must equal BD in order to fulfil (46) which indicates the condition under which the introduction of the rate of customs duty does not adversely affect the home economy.

The bigger the difference between the price of the local goods, reached without imports, and the price of foreign goods, the smaller the reduction in the price of the foreign goods needs to be, which simultaneously follows and justifies the introduction of customs duty. If in accordance with Figure 5, $p' - p = OC$, the reduction in price of r at a rate of customs duty of OB'' should equal $B''D''$; however for $p' - p = OC'$ it should equal only EB''.

If the reduction in price, r, of the foreign goods following the introduction of customs duty, z. does not reach the level indicated in (46) or in the construction of Figure 5, then the customs duty is of national economic disadvantage; the producers of the local goods will receive a subsidy paid for by the consumers of the goods in the form of the customs duty. Under certain circumstances the support of a branch of industry in economic difficulties can be justified in the same manner as can the support of parts of the population with emergency help in times of flooding or other disasters. A negligible national economic disadvantage through customs duty can, because it is not felt directly, be accepted in view of taxation policies. But only when the price reduction of foreign goods following the introduction of customs duty reaches above the amount given in (46), will it be of national economic benefit.

The answer to the question whether the introduction of a given rate of customs duty is recommended, depends on the correct assertion of the probable reduction in price of the foreign goods. If prior to the introduction of the customs duty a unit profit of g was made, then, after reduction of the price by r, this profit will diminish to $g - r$. The imported quantity is in accordance with earlier calculations $n(p' - p - z + r) - \alpha$ or, when using once more the earlier formula $p' = \alpha - z \alpha_1 a/n$, introducing the price of the local goods without imports $= n(p' - p - z + r)/2\alpha_1$. Thereby the foreign country is left, at a rate of customs duty z and a price reduction r, with a profit for the import of:

$$G = n(p' - p - z + r)(g - r)/2\alpha_1$$

which becomes a maximum for:

$$r = (g - p' + p + z)/2. \tag{47}$$

If this amount for r is substituted into (45), with the abbreviation $p' = \alpha - 2\alpha_1 a/n$, then the level of national economic utility of the increased rate of customs duty is:

$$N = n\{p' - p(g - p' + p + z) + (g - p' + p + z)^2/4 - z^2\}/4\alpha_1$$

which becomes a maximum at:

$$z = p'/3 - (p - g)/3. \tag{48}$$

The most advantageous rate of customs duty therefore equals one-third of the difference between the price which the local goods would reach without import, and the price at which the foreign goods could be supplied without any profit to the producer. The national utility from this most favourable rate of customs duty is:

$$N' = n\{(g + p' - p)^2 - 3(p' - p)^2\}/12\alpha_1. \qquad (49)$$

This becomes zero when

$$g = 0.73 \, (p' - p). \qquad (50)$$

If this profit is not obtained abroad prior to the introduction of the customs duty, then, following the introduction of the duty, the import price cannot be reduced sufficiently to allow the customs duty to become economically favourable.

It may be mentioned here that *the most favourable rate of customs duty, equation (48), is a third of the blocking rate,* that is, of that rate of duty by which all imports should be stopped; because when (47) for the value r, which indicates the level of import, is introduced, the import is obtained at:

$$n(g + p' - p - z)/4\alpha_1$$

which turns to zero for $z = p' - (p - g)$. *A blocking rate of customs duty surpasses therefore the level of the most favourable rate of customs duty threefold and is thus most unfavourable.*

Even if the difficult problems of customs duty policy have not been exhaustively dealt with above, these results have nevertheless illustrated very important conditions. They show that the most favourable rate of customs duty depends on the difference in price at which the local good would be available without import, and the price at which the foreign supplier could deliver goods without profit margin; that however, even at this most favourable rate of customs duty, a national economic profit can only be achieved when the foreign country, prior to the imposition of duty, has obtained a sufficiently big profit.

18. Formation of Prices for Indivisible Goods

Indivisible goods are valued by persons who own or wish to obtain them, according to personal preference differing from one individual to another. Everyone who owns such goods will have to be clear about the lowest price at which he or she would sell them, while everyone who wishes to buy these goods has to contemplate the limit of the price up to which he or she would maintain their interest in a purchase. In general, n persons who own the goods will value them at n different prices of A_1 up to A_n, and likewise m buyers will be interested at prices of B_1 up to B_m. In accordance with these estimates, a transfer of goods will only be possible between those buyers and owners whose assumed valuation B is equal to or higher than the assumed valuation A. The price P agreed in the first sales transaction will, as a rule, be higher than the minimum A which the owner may accept if need be, but lower than the maximum B to which the buyer will agree. The achieved price P now causes all owners who were earlier inclined to sell more cheaply to increase their price demands, while in contrast, those owners who wanted to maintain a higher price will lower their expectations somewhat. The difference between the lowest demand, A_1, and the highest, A_n, will thus decrease following the first sale. In the same manner the interested buyers will, after initially being prepared to pay a higher price than P now lower their offers, while those who had not been inclined to buy at price P will now slightly raise their offers, so that the difference between the lowest offer, B_1, and the highest, B_m, will be smaller. The first sales contract has therefore a levelling effect on the valuations of both sellers and buyers and simplifies the following contracts which will lead more and more to the formation of a definite market price. Understandably, however, the price formation for indivisible goods escapes mathematical treatment.

PART 2

The Production of Goods

19. Human Labour

Goods offered in nature for the fulfilment of human needs are not usually accessible without the investment of effort to obtain them. Human activity performed for a useful effect is termed labour. In individual cases the performance of a certain activity allows human beings immediate pleasure, as for instance in the case of playing games and sport, or in the execution of artistic or scientific work. In general, however, work is felt to be a curse or nuisance to which human beings subject themselves only in return for pleasure.

It must be possible to measure the units of pleasure and of the nuisance of work with the same gauge. The misery of work has to be interpreted as negative pleasure which can be balanced by a positive pleasure of equal absolute degree. Just as the extent of the pleasure grows more slowly than the quantity of consumption, so on the other hand, the extent of the misery of work grows faster than the 'quantity' of completed work. A daily task taking four hours appears little trouble while a daily task stretched to four times that period causes misery bordering on the unbearable. This amounts to the effort equation which indicates the extent of the work effort, m, depending on the daily working hours, t, and is formulated in general terms as

$$m = \psi(t).$$

If working hours are introduced as abscissae and work effort as ordinates, the shape of a curve is demonstrated in Figure 6 by line mmm.

Similarly, when naming the first derivative of the utility function 'marginal utility', the first derivvative of the effort equation can be named the *marginal disutility*.

In exchange for wages paid for work of p' per working hour, that is $p't$ for t working hours per pay, a quantity, x, of consumer goods can be obtained which allow utility of $g = F(x)$. If the price per unit

Figure 6

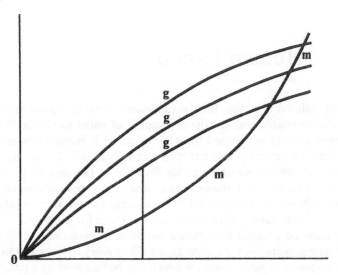

of consumer goods is p″ then the quantity exchangeable for the wages of a day's work is $x = t(p'/p'')$, which means that utility is:

$$g = F(tp'/p'').$$

In Figure 6, the curves Og commencing from the start of the coordinates depict utility for various price ratios where working hours are represented as abscissae. It is realized that the surplus of pleasure over the trouble of work becomes largest at a certain level of t, derived from the equation:

$$u = F(tp'/p'') - \psi(t)$$

by differentiation with respect to t, giving:

$$(p'/p'')F'(tp'/p'') = \psi'(t)$$

or, because $x = t(p'/p'')$:

$$\frac{F'(x)}{p''} = \frac{\psi'(t)}{p'}. \tag{51}$$

This means that *the priceworthiness of pleasure must equal the price-worthiness of work*. That is exactly the same condition that was found to apply to the exchange of two goods; in fact this is nothing else than the exchange of pleasure for work.

If for further demonstration one adopts for the utility function the formula

$$F(x) = \gamma x - \gamma_1 x^2$$

and for the effort equation the formula:

$$\psi(t) = \beta t + \beta_1 t^2$$

then the surplus of pleasure over effort of work equals:

$$u = (\gamma t p'/p'') - (p'/p'')^2 \gamma_1 t^2 - \beta t - \beta_1 t^2$$

from which the most favourable level of daily work is:

$$t' = \frac{\gamma p'/p'' - \beta}{2(\beta_1 + \gamma_1 p'^2/p''^2)}. \tag{52}$$

The more the pay p' per working hour increases, the greater is the incentive to work, and the longer the most favourable daily work period becomes. However, the increase in working time reaches its limit at a certain price ratio which is found by differentiation of (52) with respect to p'/p'':

$$\frac{p'}{p''} = \frac{\beta}{\gamma} + \left\{ \frac{\beta^2}{\gamma^2} + \frac{\beta_1}{\gamma_1} \right\}^{0.5}. \tag{53}$$

At this rate of pay, which could be called the *incentive rate* because an incentive to increase the daily work period exists up to this rate, the limit to the daily work period is as follows:

$$t'' = \frac{(\gamma/4\gamma_1)(\beta^2/\gamma^2 + \beta_1/\gamma_1)^{0.5}}{\beta^2/\gamma^2 + \beta_1/\gamma_1 + (\beta/\gamma)(\beta^2/\gamma^2 + \beta_1/\gamma_1)^{0.5}}. \tag{54}$$

With an increase in the hourly rate above the level indicated in (53), a shorter work period suffices to reach the maximum pleasure surplus. With a further increase in the hourly rate the most favourable work period slowly decreases and approaches asymptotically the value 0. When determining the most favourable period of daily work it has to be kept in mind that for the maintenance of life a certain minimum x_0 of consumer goods will be necessary. In determining the daily working hours necessary to ensure this minimum requirement, then at least $t'p'/p'' = x_0$, or after introducing the level t' of (52):

$$x_0 = \frac{\gamma(p'/p'')^2 - \beta(p'/p'')}{2\{\beta_1 + \gamma_1(p'/p'')^2\}}$$

from which it follows that, to secure the absolute minimum sustenance, the price ratio between the hourly pay rate and the price of the consumer good must at least be:

$$\frac{p'}{p''} = \frac{\beta}{2\gamma - 4\gamma_1 x_0}[\,1 + \{\,1 + \frac{4\beta_1 x_0}{\beta^2}(2\gamma - 4\gamma_1 x_0)\,\}^{0.5}]. \tag{55}$$

This rate of pay, while adhering to the most favourable daily working hours, at which the minimally necessary earnings can still be obtained, may be called the *sufficiency rate of pay*. If the rate of pay slips below this sufficiency rate, the most favourable working hours at which as big a surplus as possible of pleasure over toil can be reached, can no longer be maintained. Working hours have to be extended beyond the most favourable level in order to make a mere living, so that a ratio of $t = x_0 p''/p'$ results.

If the rate of pay, p', continues to decrease, a period of work becomes necessary where the toil of work equals the pleasure exchangeable for the wages, which corresponds to the point where the effort curve and the pleasure curve in Figure 6 meet. In this situation the following result is obtained:

$$\gamma x_0 - \gamma_1 x_0^2 = \beta t + \beta_1 t^2$$

or, because $x_0 = tp'/p''$ it follows that:

$$\gamma(tp'/p'') - \gamma_1(tp'/p'')^2 = \beta t + \beta_1 t^2$$

from which the daily work is:

$$t''' = \frac{\gamma p'/p'' - \beta}{\beta_1 + \gamma_1 (p'/p'')^2}. \tag{56}$$

This amounts, as can be seen from a comparison with (52), to double the working period at which the greatest surplus of pleasure relative to the rate of pay is obtained. Working hours must be extended to this level when $t'''p'/p'' = x_0$ or, after introducing the expression from (56) for t''', when:

$$x_0 = \frac{\gamma(p'/p'')^2 - \beta(p'/p'')}{\beta_1 + \gamma_1(p'/p'')^2}$$

from which:

$$\frac{p'}{p''} = \frac{\beta}{2\gamma - 2\gamma_1 x_0} [1 + \{ 1 + \frac{2\beta_1 x_0}{\beta^2} (2\gamma - 2\gamma_1 x_0) \}^{0.5}]. \tag{57}$$

This lowest rate of pay is the *emergency rate of pay*. A lowering of the hourly pay rate below the emergency rate would necessitate an extension of the working period to ensure bare survival, at which the toil would be perceived as so painful that the pleasure of life would not represent any compensation, so that life would not seem worth living. A human being would only expose himself to a further extension of working hours, at a rate of pay which remains below the emergency rate, so long as he can maintain hope for an improvement of conditions.

If, for example, figures are introduced into the formulae established, for a clearer demonstration, with $\alpha = 2$, $\alpha_1 = 1/800$, $\beta = 4$, $\beta_1 = 1$, $p'' = 2$ and $x_0 = 120$, then the emergency rate of pay comes to 18.4, for which a working period of 13 hours needs to be invested. The sufficiency rate of pay comes to 26.24 with a working period of 9.15 hours and the incentive rate of pay equals 60.8 with a working period of 13.2 hours. The supply of labour will thus commence at the emergency wages of 18.4 per working hour, and a working period of 13 hours. *If the hourly pay rate rises above the emergency rate of pay, the supply of labour from the individual worker decreases.* If the worker maintained the same hours of work at a higher pay rate as under the condition of emergency wages, then he would reach a higher daily wage, but the surplus of pleasure over toil would decrease compared to a situation where he limited his efforts to

Figure 7

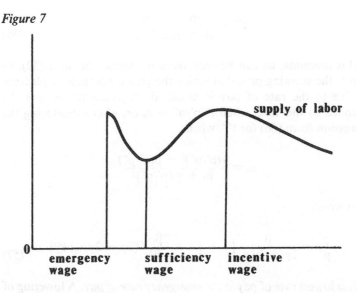

obtaining just sufficient means to pay for the bare minimum of
sustenance and in turn shortened the daily working period. This
truth has long been recognized in the circles of labourers whose
wages lie between the emergency rate of pay and the sufficiency rate.
These workers do not demand *a rise in their daily wages while
maintaining the long working hours, but a decrease in working hours
while maintaining the daily wage.*

The decrease in the supply of labour on the part of the individual
worker will continue with an increasing hourly pay rate until the
sufficiency rate has been reached. If a further increase in the hourly
rate occurs, then the incentive to prolong the working period will
develop, and the supply of labour will increase. This increase of the
supply of labour will continue at a rising hourly pay rate until the
incentive rate has been reached where a further increase in the
hourly rate once again leads to a decrease in the supply of labour. In
Figure 7 the supply of labour is depicted whereby the pay rate per
hour relative to the price of a pleasure unit, p'/p'', has been introduced as abscissae and the respective working periods as ordinates.

The seeming contradiction, that with the increase of the price the
supply of labour will decrease, disappears as soon as the supply of
labour is not looked at from the point of the individual labourer but
from the overall sum of labour by a larger number of workers. The

minimum amount which pays for the cost of living is not the same for all labourers; it is for instance higher for the breadwinner of a family than for a single person. Besides, the drudgery of work will be assessed differently by different individuals, as a lesser effort by the healthy and willing than by the lazy and weak. But primarily the difference in the kinds of work to be performed will lead to a very varied representation of the effort equation. Every individual will – if subconsciously – make up the drudgery equation for the various labours from which to choose in a different way, where the same chores will be appraised by different workers differently. With some chores a moderate effort is often not looked upon as drudgery, but appreciated as an immediate pleasure so that the effort equation takes the form of $m = -\beta t + \beta_1 t^2$.

Every individual will prefer among all the chores those which can be performed in accordance with his personal ability and training and which, in consideration of the rate of pay and after an estimate of the toil, offer the greatest surplus in pleasure. If therefore the hourly pay rate for a certain job is increased, other workers will turn their attention towards it and give up their earlier occupation because with the new rate of pay a greater surplus in pleasure can be obtained. If, following the pay increase, the supply of labour from the individual labourer decreases, then by way of added interest from the new group of workers, the sum of labour supplied has increased. The function represented by the sum of supply of labour relative to the rate of pay will therefore generally show a steady increase in the supply of labour relative to the increase in pay.

Finally we may consider a case where the worker has sources of income at his disposal other than wages, be this income from property or interest from investments. If this income allows for pleasure of F (a) then the pleasure will be increased by the addition of wages to $F(a + tp'/p'')$, this means that by putting into effect the formulae for the utility function and the effort equation a surplus of pleasure is obtained:

$$u = \gamma(a + tp'/p'') - \gamma_1(a + tp'/p'') - \beta t - \beta_1 t^2$$

which reaches a maximum at:

$$t' = \frac{(\gamma - 2\gamma_1 a)(p'/p'') - \beta}{2\{\beta_1 + \gamma_1(p'/p'')^2\}}.$$

This becomes zero if

$$\frac{\beta}{p'} = \frac{\gamma - 2\gamma_1 a}{p''}.$$ (58)

Somebody who can enjoy a quantity of pleasure, a, will limit themselves to this pleasure and thus become a *pensioner* if they cannot reach a higher rate of pay for their work than the rate p' given in (58).

20.   Price Formation in the Production of Goods

Industrial goods in their natural appearance are called *raw materials* but also *natural products*. The preparation of raw materials for use is often initiated and effected by human labour, as for instance in agriculture and forestry, or it occurs completely free of human interference so that it is limited to the activities of gathering and collecting of the readily existing natural product. But even in this latter situation it is often necessary to carry out extensive preparatory work before one can proceed to obtain the natural products, as for example in mining, and only in a few cases does this ○T'rst labour effort lead to the direct obtaining of the goods, as for example in gathering the fruit in the forest, guano etc. Obviously these last examples show the simplest way of obtaining goods which is to be interpreted as an exchange of labour for natural goods. If one disregards the never quite avoidable lesser efforts and costs, then the labour unit supplies directly a definite number of units of goods.

If for example in an hour z kilos of wild berries are gathered which will be sold at the price p'' per kilo, then the working hour is paid by $p' = p''z$. If the utility function of the wild berries is F (x), then their price must be $p' = F'(x)$; then the pay for the labour, if its effort equation is $\psi(t)$, equals $p'' = \psi'(t)$. So $\psi'(t) = zF'(x)$ is reached, or, as $z = p'/p''$:

$$\frac{\psi'(p)}{p'} = \frac{F'(x)}{p''}. \tag{59}$$

This is the fundamental law of exchange formulated in Chapter 4, according to which the priceworthiness of the berries must equal the priceworthiness of the labour.

If few people gather berries and the harvest is small, then the berries can be bought only in small quantities and their level of usefulness, i.e. their price, is high. The gatherers obtain high wages for their labour, therefore other persons will be attracted to the same occupation, so that the supply of berries will increase and their price as well as the pay for the gatherers will decrease. This development will continue until a price is reached at which the gatherer cannot obtain a larger surplus of pleasure than with any other kind of work. The shift of workers from other occupations will not take place without counter effects because the decrease in the quantity of labour in those other areas of work will be followed by a decrease in production, and due to this an increase in the price of the goods which must simultaneously cause an increase in wages. If it is supposed that the gathering of berries is a new occupation additional to the earlier existing jobs, then those workers occupied with gathering berries will be drawn from other areas of occupation, which will not be possible without a general increase in wages and following that an increase of prices for goods.

For the price formation of consumer goods, apart from the condition formulated in Chapter 14 according to which their priceworthiness must equal the priceworthiness of all other consumer goods, there exists therefore the condition that for their production, workers must be able to reach the same surplus of pleasure as can be reached in other occupations within their abilities.

If the pay rate for simple manual labour which can be executed without prior training and support, which is what is presently under discussion, lies below the sufficiency rate, then to obtain the minimum survival rate, the number of working hours has to be extended beyond the most favourable length. For all the different occupations for which the sufficiency pay rate has not yet been reached, the toil factor by which a living is made must be identical. If this were not the case, then additional workers would turn to those job areas in which the minimum survival rate of pay could be obtained with less struggle, and depress wages further until in this job, too, the same input of effort would have to be made as for the others where, due to the decrease in labour supply, wages have risen in the meantime.

If this constant figure is k, for the toil and the effort equation $\beta t + \beta_1 t^2$, then $k = \beta t + \beta_1 t^2$. By this the number of daily working hours is indicated and therefore also the quantity of goods produced by a worker per day is zt if z is the quantity of goods produced per hour. If, further, c is the daily wage necessary to cover the minimum daily cost of living, then the price of producing the goods must be

$p = c/zt$. If the value $t = c/pz$ derived from this is introduced into the effort equation, then we obtain:

$$k = \beta(c/zp) + \beta_1(c/zp)^2$$

from which is obtained the production price of the goods at:

$$p = \frac{\beta c}{2zk}\{1 + (1 + 4\beta_1 k/\beta^2)^{0.5}\}. \tag{60}$$

According to this equation, the production price of goods is determined such that in all occupational areas the minimally necessary daily wage c can be obtained with an equal input of toil k, so that the pleasure surplus or state of comfort, u, is equal for all varieties of labour.

If, however, conditions in the labour market have improved to such a degree for the labourer that the sufficiency rate of pay (equation 55) is surpassed, then he will intensify his activity to such a level; that is, extend the number of working hours so that a maximum of pleasure surplus will be reached. This maximum must again have the same figure u for all areas of activity, which depends on the conditions in the labour market. At the rate of daily pay pzt and a price p'' per unit of consumer goods, a quantity x of consumer goods equal to pzt/p'' can be obtained so that for the pleasure equation, $F(x) = \gamma x - \gamma_1 x^2$, the following pleasure surplus is reached:

$$u = \gamma(ztp/p'') - \gamma_1(2tp/p'')^2 - \beta t - \beta_1 t^2.$$

In this situation the working period t is set in such a way that it allows u to be as large as possible, which will be the case when:

$$t = \frac{\gamma pzp'' - \beta p''^2}{2(\beta_1 p''^2 + \gamma_1 p^2 z^2)}. \tag{61}$$

If this value of t is substituted into the expression for the pleasure surplus, then:

$$u = \frac{(\gamma pz - \beta p'')^2}{4(\beta_1 p''^2 + \gamma_1 p^2 z^2)}$$

from which the price of production for the goods is:

$$p = \frac{\gamma \beta p''}{z(\gamma^2 - 4\gamma_1 u)} \left[1 + \left\{ 1 + \frac{1}{\gamma^2 \beta^2} (\gamma^2 - 4\gamma_1 u)(4\beta_1 u - \beta^2) \right\}^{0.5} \right]. \tag{62}$$

In a borderline case where the sufficiency rate of pay is reached by way of the price of the goods, both equations (60) and (62) will give an identical value. If, as in an earlier example, the following values are introduced, $\gamma = 2$, $\gamma_1 = 1/800$, $\beta = 4$, $\beta_1 = 1$, $p'' = 2$ and further $z = 4$, then to satisfy the bare minimum survival needs a quantity $x_0 = 120$ units of consumer goods which can therefore be obtained at a daily pay rate $c = p''x_0 = 240$; then, according to equation (55), the sufficiency rate of pay per working hour is $p' = 26.24$, i.e. equalling the price for the unit of goods because $z = 4$, $p = 6.56$. At this rate of the sufficiency rate of pay the daily period of work according to equation (52) amounts to 9.15 hours from which a toil level $k = 120$ arises, while the pleasure level $g = 2(120) - (1/800)(120)^2 = 222$ and thus the pleasure surplus results in $u = g - k = 102$.

If in equation (62) the value for $u = 102$ or in equation (60) the value $k = 120$, then both must arrive at the figure 6.56 for p. As long as the generally obtainable pleasure surplus for the workers is below 102, equation (60) must be used for the calculation of the production price for goods. If, however, the comfort factor has increased to such a level that the pleasure surplus has risen above 102, then the price of goods must be calculated in accordance with equation (62). If due to the conditions in the labour market a pleasure surplus of only 80 has become obtainable, they should, for the purpose of earning the bare minimum survival wages for which $x_0 = 120$ units of consumer goods are necessary, i.e. a pleasure of $2(120) - (1/800)(120)^2 = 222$, a toil effort of $k = 222 - 80 = 142$ would have to be made so that, according to equation (60), the price p for goods would equal 5.92. If however the comfort level of the labourer had improved so far that a pleasure surplus $u = 160$ was reached, then, according to equation (61), the price of goods $p = 8.34$. The workers would, in case 1, receive an hourly pay rate of $4(5.92) = 23.68$, and, to obtain the minimum necessary survival wages of $c = 240$, would have to work $240/23.68 = 10.02$ hours. In case 2, the hourly rate of pay would come to $4(8.34) = 33.36$ and, according to equation (61), the number of working hours be extended to 10.9.

In our previous investigations the dependence of the production price of goods on the level of pleasure surplus which can be obtained by labourers, was followed up. The extent of the pleasure surplus which can be reached by the workers depends in turn on the supply of labour and the demand for the produced goods. If the utility of the produced goods is $\alpha x - \alpha_1 x^2$ then someone who purchases a quantity x' at a price of p will obtain, according to Chapter 14, a priceworthiness of his holdings of:

$$w' = (\alpha - 2\alpha_1 x')/p.$$

Thus when he can purchase at such a priceworthiness, his demand is:

$$x' = (\alpha - pw')/2\alpha_1.$$

Someone else who can, in accordance with his income, purchase at a priceworthiness w'' will limit his demand to:

$$x'' = (\alpha - pw'')/2\alpha_1.$$

If n persons express a demand for the merchandise and are able to purchase at an average priceworthiness of w, then the sum of their demand amounts to:

$$N = n(\alpha - pw)/2\alpha_1. \tag{63}$$

This demand, which corresponds to the requirements for a year, is juxtaposed with the supply. In the case that the income through wages of the labourers lies below the sufficiency rate of pay, every labourer will produce a quantity of goods c/p in one day or at a rate of 300 working days per annum 300c/p. By a number m of workers a quantity of goods 300mc/p will therefore be produced for supply. By equating the supply and the demand indicated in equation (63), the number of workers is arrived at who have to be employed in the respective manufacturing plant, to arrive at the production price p through which the workers reach the level of pleasure surplus which corresponds to the conditions in the labour market, at:

$$m = np(\alpha - pw)/600\alpha_1 c. \tag{64}$$

If, however, the sufficiency rate of pay is reached or surpassed, then m workers produce during one year a quantity of goods of

300mzt whereby the number of working hours t is determined in equation (61). If this value is introduced for t and the quantity of goods obtained equals the demand indicated in equation (63), the number of workers who have to be employed in order to limit the price of goods at the level p is:

$$m = \frac{n(\beta_1 p''^2 + \gamma_1 p^2 z^2)(\alpha - pw)}{300\alpha_1 z(\gamma pzp'' - \beta p''^2)}. \tag{65}$$

Equations (64) and (65) give the same result for a number m of workers in a borderline case in which exactly the same sufficiency wages are reached with the price of goods p.

If for instance the utility function of the goods were $x - x^2/1000$, $\alpha = 1$ and $\alpha_1 = 1/1000$ and, further, the priceworthiness at which $n = 1,000,000$ persons were able to purchase, and on average $w = 1/8$, the absolute minimum survival rate of daily pay c would equal 240; and further, as previously assumed, $z = 4, p'' = 2, \gamma = 2$, $\gamma_1 = 1/800, \beta = 4, \beta_1 = 1$, then, at a product price of $p = 6.56$, as earlier calculated, the sufficiency rate of pay would actually be obtained. Application of both (64) and (65) gives in this case the result that the number of workers to be employed $m = 6560$. If however the sufficiency rate of pay under the prevailing conditions of the labour market could not be obtained and only a price of $p = 5$ were reached, then according to equation (64) a number $m = 10,418$ should be employed; but if a product price $p = 7$ were paid at which the sufficiency rate of pay is exceeded, then according to formula (65) only $m = 4323$ workers could find employment. At a product price of $p = 5$ the number of working hours has to be increased to 12 hours to gain the minimum daily pay rate $c = 240$ to cover basic needs whereby a pleasure level $g = 222$ at an input of toil $= 192$ is invested, i.e. an excess in pleasure of 30 is achieved; in contrast, at the produce price $p = 7$, according to equation (61), a number of working hours $t = 9.64$ needs to be invested at which a daily pay rate $= 270$, meaning a pleasure level of 247 with an input of toil effort $= 132$, and therefore a pleasure surplus of 115 has been achieved.

The achievable pleasure surplus in the production of any given goods for the workers employed in the production depends, according to these explanations, on the number of workers employed. If all existing workers were equally able to work in any kind of production plant, then their total number would be distributed over individual industries in such a way that the same measure of surplus pleasure is achieved. The level of this surplus pleasure would depend on the number of workers available and on the demand created by the number and affluence of consumers as well as on the usefulness of the produced goods. How the state of contentment of the individual worker varies due to the variance in their personal ability will be discussed further in Chapter 25 after the remaining factors having a bearing on the matter have been considered.

In addition to these observations it needs to be kept in mind that for the production of goods, as a rule, a larger or smaller number of raw materials and other substances are needed, the price of which must be added to the wages costs. If to the cost of the ready-made product an amount z' is added to the unit price p' for raw materials and additional components or substances, and further z'' units added to unit price p'' etc. up to z_n units added to unit price p_n, and the interest of the investment capital added to each product is ki, wages p_0, general overheads u and the profit margin for the producer g, then the price per unit of goods will amount to

$$p = p'z' + p''z'' + \ldots + p_n z_n + p_0 + u + g + ki.$$

If this formula for p is substituted into the 'equation for demand' (63), the result will be:

$$N = \frac{nw}{2\alpha_1} \{ \frac{\alpha}{w} - (p'z' + p''z'' + \ldots + p_n z_n + p_0 + u + g + ki) \}$$

$$(66)$$

and the demand for the individual raw materials, components and additional substances derive from the following:

$$N' = \frac{nwz'}{2\alpha_1} \{ \frac{\alpha}{w} - (p'z' + p''z'' + \ldots + p_n z_n + u + g + ki) \}.$$

$$(67)$$

Because, as a rule, raw materials and materials added to them are utilized for the production of a number of goods, (67) gives the demand for individual categories of goods, and by adding these up, the total demand for the respective raw materials can be found. Demand for a given raw material is, according to this, dependent on the prices of a great many; strictly speaking, it is dependent on the prices of all other goods. As the price in turn depends on the extent of the demand, the formation of prices for all goods is most intricately interconnected, which in the business scene can understandably be unravelled only in continuous, careful attempts, and only partially at that.

21. Preparatory and Manufacturing Work

For the greater utilization of human labour, tools, machines and auxiliary equipment of the widest variety are harnessed, with the help of which the execution of work is made easier, but for the production of which a considerable input of work and effort is often necessary. The *preparatory* work or labour which is expended on the making of tools, apparatus and machinery, on the construction of buildings and roads, on the training and education of workers, does not usually serve just one manufacturing work process, but is done for a larger number of work processes following one another. If the total number of the work projects, the preparatory as well as the producing ones, are closely timed, then the preparatory work can in a simple way be proportionally added to the actual part of the work which can be done by dividing the preparatory work by the number of manufacturing work projects. In most instances, however, the manufacturing work is spread over a longer period of time so that the preparatory work done before the commencement of the series of work projects is only fully taken advantage of over a period of time.

The resource created by the preparatory work effort turns into capital, more exactly into an asset, i.e., in accordance with the terminology established in Chapter 2, into goods which cannot be used up in a single instance of consumption, but the utilization of which is tied to a certain time span.

If an amount of money A is necessary for the preparatory work, the establishment of the asset, and if the resource thus produced has a useful duration of n years, then the annual amount k should be calculated by which the investment capital including interest is repaid in n years. At an annual interest rate i of the first annual amount k, repayment is served by $k - Ai$, of the second annual amount $(k - Ai)(1 + i)$, of the n-th annual amount $(k - Ai)(1 + i)^{n-1}$. If the sum of these individual repayments equals A the

107

result will be:

$$k = \frac{Ai(1+i)^n}{(1+i)^n - 1}. \tag{68}$$

The annual amount which will with regular interest payments repay the investment capital A in n years, can be divided in two, of which the first part, $k' = Ai$, covers interest payments and the second

$$k'' = Ai/\{(1+i)^n - 1\}$$

can be used to accumulate the needed renewal capital in n years. For an indefinitely long duration this last part, k'', will turn to zero.

The figure with which the investment capital has to be multiplied to arrive at the amount needed annually to cover the interest and repayment may be called *repayment interest*. The ratio, if i' represents this repayment interest, is therefore $k = Ai'$, resulting in:

$$i' = \frac{i(1+i)^n}{(1+i)^n - 1}. \tag{69}$$

The more elaborate the preparatory work is, in other words, the larger is the investment capital A, and the smaller will be the work effort of the manufacturing labour. The costs of this actual production work, which are named running costs B, therefore represent a function of the investment capital which may be set at $f(A)$.

The total annual expenditure of a manufacturing plant, which consists of the sum of the running costs and the payment of interest and repayment of the capital investment, must, if calculated correctly, become a minimum. For the sum $S = B + Ai'$ or:

$$S = f(A) + Ai'$$

the minimum is obtained if:

$$f'(A) + i' = 0. \tag{70}$$

This basic equation of the manufacturing plant therefore is: The first derivative of the function which represents the dependence of the

Figure 8

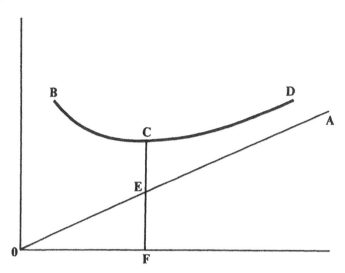

running costs on the investment capital must equal the repayment interest which is necessary for the investment capital. This condition, free from its mathematical mode of expression is: the level of the investment capital has to be calculated high enough until by way of its increase by another capital unit the decrease in the running costs caused by this equals the level of the repayment interest deriving from the newly invested capital unit.

The basic equation of the manufacturing plant can be graphically demonstrated in a simple manner. If the extent of the investment capital in Figure 8 is measured on the abscissa, then the interest of the investment capital may be measured by the ordinates which rise in a straight line OA from the starting point of the coordinates. If the running costs $B = f(A)$ relative to the investment capital are introduced above this 'interest line' so that CE shows the running costs at an investment capital of OF, then at the lowest point of the curve representing the running costs, BCD, one arrives at the condition for the most useful level of investment capital which therefore must equal the abscissa OF at this point.

The cost of preparatory work put into furthering a worker's personal talents must be repaid by way of a surcharge on the rate of pay. If, for instance, the expenses of the education and training of a worker, including all costs for his food, clothing etc. from his birth up to the age of 18 years, amounted to 2000 Marks inclusive of calculated compound interest, and if the performance of labour from this point in time to age 50 could be counted on, then according to equation (67) at a calculation of 5 per cent interest the following repayment formula would have to form the basis:

$$i' = \frac{(0.05)(1.05)^{32}}{(1.05)^{32} - 1} = 0.0633.$$

The annual repayment amount for the investment capital of 2000 Marks would therefore have to be $(0.0633)\,(2000) = 126.6$ Marks which amounts to 42 pfennigs per working day at an annual average of 300 working days. A higher civil servant who does not receive a salary until the age of 30 and whose education and training from his birth cost 50,000 Marks including interest and compound interest, would in a career of 30 years have to base the calculation for the repayment of the capital accumulated in his person on an amount of $(0.0654)\,(50,000) = 3270$ Marks.

It should be mentioned here, by the way, that with the furthering of personal talents, i.e. with the increase in personal value, expectations of the living standard rightfully also rise, so that a higher rate of pay which only suffices to cover the costs of education and training will not satisfy the better-educated worker.

In the same way as the costs of personal training, the costs for work put into establishing relevant installations can be raised and added to the rate of pay. The small, self-employed craftsman does not charge the costs of his tools or even his workshop separately when determining the prices of goods manufactured by him, but as a surcharge on the daily rate of pay. In larger and more-developed manufacturing plants, however, repayment costs of the investment capital will be accounted and calculated separately of wages costs for the actual manufacture. In addition to the costs of the manufacture and of raw materials and additional components and substances for a quantity Q of the produced goods, expenses for the repayment of the investment capital of Ai/Q will arise.

22. Business Profit

For work places which require the cooperation of a number of workers, whose activities are based on the utilization of capital, a manager is needed who looks after the economic management of the plant. As a rule the manager is the owner of the capital invested in the workplace, or at least a part-owner of the capital. It is well known that there are numerous examples of cases where the workforce within a workplace as a cooperative took on the responsibilities of management. But even if this is so, in his economic role the manager is always seen as a third entity apart from workers and capitalists. The entrepreneur has, above all, as the highest-ranking worker in the business, the right to a salary; secondly, he will have to be rewarded for the risks which he accepts by taking on responsibility and liability for possible losses by way of an appropriate profit.

Due to the profit margin, g, to the businessman the production price of goods rises to $p + g$ and the demand which is a function of the price, will become $F(p + g)$. The total profit

$$G = gF(p + g)$$

reaches, for a certain level of the profit margin per unit, its maximum level. To obtain the most favourable profit margin, differentiate with respect to g, to get:

$$g = -F(p + g)/F'(p + g). \qquad (71)$$

This is the *basic equation for profit.*

If in Figure 9 the ordinates of curve ACB represent the demand, $F(p + g)$, the abscissae being the profit margin, g, then the most favourable profit margin OD is the abscissae of point C of the demand curve which is situated in the centre of the tangent ECF. The basic equation or profit demands that *the profit margin equals the sub-tangent of the demand curve.*

If, for instance, the utility function of the produced goods is set at

111

Figure 9

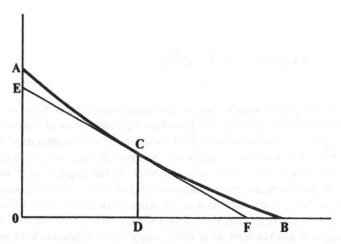

$\alpha a - \alpha_1 a^2$, then for n buyers of the goods who can purchase on an average at a priceworthiness of w, the demand in accordance with equation (63) is given by:

$$F(p + g) = n\{\alpha - (p + g)w\}/2\alpha_1$$

resulting in

$$G = gF(p + g) = ng\{\alpha - (p + g)w\}/2\alpha_1.$$

From this, one arrives at the most favourable level of the profit margin:

$$g = \frac{\alpha}{2w} - \frac{p}{2} \tag{72}$$

at which the profit level reached equals:

$$G = n(\alpha - pw)^2/8\alpha_1 w. \tag{73}$$

The profit therefore becomes larger, the larger is the number of buyers of the produced goods and the customers' level of affluence, or in turn, the smaller is the priceworthiness at which they are still able to buy.

The profit will also be larger, the larger is the value α of the produced goods. The manager must in this context make sure, for his own advantage, of the best possible quality of the produced goods. But with the better quality of goods the production price will certainly increase so that α can be equal to a given function φ(p) of the production price. This must become a maximum to the advantage of the entrepreneur, φ(p) − pw, which will occur at:

$$\phi'(p) = w. \tag{74}$$

The decisive condition for the level of quality of goods is indicated in this simple equation. *The first derivative of the equation which expresses the dependence of the value on the production price must equal the average priceworthiness at which the consumers can purchase the goods.* The quality of the goods must therefore be improved in proportion to the level of affluence of the group of consumers; it may, however, not surpass a certain level in consideration of the profit to be made.

It is further realized that it is of great importance to the producer to lower the production price, p, of goods as far as possible because this will not only increase the profit surcharge per unit but also the turnover. Initially there exists a great incentive for the producer to achieve a very high standard in the production of goods, but this also explains the attempt to keep interest on the capital and wage costs at a minimum. The often-stressed opposition between capital and labour proves an at least inaccurate interpretation of the facts. *It is not the capitalist who takes a hostile position towards the labourer, but it is the manager using capital and labour who oppresses the capitalist as well as the labourer.*

But it has already been stressed that the businessman's profit relies on the affluence of his customers whose numbers are made up of businessmen, merchants, capitalists and workers. A reduction of interest, wages and salaries reduces the average affluence of the customers on whom the businessman depends. There are for this very reason limits for the businessman below which the interest, wages and salaries must not fall. Investors and workers will defend their point of view and not allow their incomes to be reduced by the businessman to the level most favourable to him.

At a given interest rate and rate of pay, at given costs for the enterprise, it still needs to be remembered that the capital to be invested in the enterprise as well as the sum of the wages to be paid do not increase at the same rate as the quantity of goods produced, but that only a part of the production costs increase in proportion to the quantity of goods produced, while another part, which is called *general expenditure*, remains at the same level unrelated to the extent of production. The share of the general expenditure on each unit decreases with an increase in production. In the determination of the most favourable profit to the producer, based on the production price of the goods, the general expenditure must not be considered because only after the level of profit margin and thereby the level of sales has been decided will it be possible to determine the size of the share of general expenditure on each unit. The general expenditure, remaining unchanged, can be deducted by the businessman from profits to arrive at the net profit. If the net profit does not supply sufficient reward for the efforts of the businessman and represents an insufficient insurance premium to cover possible losses, then the business is not *profitable*. If it however pays even a small surplus after payment of wages and salaries and a reward in proportion to the responsibility taken on with regards to possible losses, then there will immediately be an influx of other businessmen interested in the relevant market.

The growth in the quantity of goods produced by new businesses will only find a market if, by reducing the profit margin for the manager, the price of goods will be lowered. The influx of additional businesses in the same area of production, the increase in production and the lowering of prices will continue until that price level for the goods has been reached at which the businessman will be compensated for his work and risks at such a low level that the incentive for other producers to join in has come to an end.

The earlier calculated most-favourable profit to the businessman can only be obtained when the area of goods and services can be operated as a *monopoly*. Wherever free competition has not been excluded, the profit for the businessman will have to sink to that very low level indicated earlier. It should however be kept in mind that that minimum profit margin, without which the business would not be profitable, nevertheless applies only to very few, or strictly speaking to only one, of the businessmen who operate under the worst conditions among the competitors. This weakest operator decides the price; if the price drops further, he will have to close the business through the continuation of which he would otherwise sustain a loss;

the result will be a reduction in supplies of these goods and an increase in price must follow. This will enable another producer to enter the market who need not be stronger than the one who went out of business.

While the businessman working under the least-favourable conditions will have to work without any real profit, all others working in more-favourable circumstances will obtain a profit which more or less exceeds the level of reward due to them relative to their work effort and risk-taking. The more favourable conditions for the businessman can be based on a better economic position in a more densely populated region or among an affluent population, or on better transport facilities, on greater capital possession which allows expansion of the enterprise, spreading the general expenditure and lowering it per unit; further, it can be based on better equipment and work processes in the production which allow for a lower production price. The most decisive factor for the development of extremely high profit lies in the last-mentioned condition. An invention which improves the production method often gives immeasurable profit, especially when the producer, by keeping it secret or protecting it by patent, can exploit the method alone. The overall business profit will be graded from the businessman with the greatest advantage of possessing the best economic opportunities, highest capital investment and personal talents, down to the one who is least endowed in all these respects, from a maximum of profit to zero. The business profit therefore develops, according to this realization, along the same lines as returns from land-holdings based on their situation and quality of soil (cf. Chapter 23). The profit obtained by the business is totally justifiable and cannot be eliminated by any means; to achieve equality of earnings one would then have to provide all producers in the same area of production with identical economic conditions, allow identical capital investment; but more than that, have to be able to give them all an identical measure of cleverness and other personal talents.

The complaints by workers made frequently and loudly about the oppression they suffer through capitalists, or more precisely about capitalists acting as entrepreneurs, should not be directed against profit itself but against that part of it which derives from the suppression of wages. It has been proven that the suppression of wages is to the advantage of the producer, but the worker in his fight for increased wages will find proportionally less opposition from the employer, the more the employer's profit is secured by circumstances which, like a favourable economic situation, high capital investment, and personal ability of the producer, are independent of rates of pay for labour. Everyone will find the worker's battle for increased wages reasonable, but the often-voiced demand by the worker for part or even all of the business profit is totally unjustifiable. Can, for example, a bricklayer who works on alterations to a house, to turn it into shops in the best shopping area of town with the chance to double its rental value, ask for higher pay than his work-mate who performs the same work on a house on the outskirts of town which proves to bring small returns? Nobody will be able to sustain this demand. Nobody can award the worker part of the profit which is obtained by the businessman. The only way to give the profit to the workers is the one adopted on a trial basis, putting a worker's co-operative in place of the manager. Even if such undertakings deserve, not only from the philanthropic point of view but also from economic considerations, the greatest success because the buying power, the economic weight of society as a whole, increases in proportion to general affluence, these failed attempts have to be seen as completely pointless. The difficulties of securing the necessary capital, of regulating the rights and duties of the participants, of enforcing the necessary variations in the supply of labour are so immense that because of these the co-operative is of necessity almost always pushed into the weakest position among the enterprises whose profit turns to zero.

23. Returns from Land

The amount of labour needed to obtain natural products varies for the same kind of good according to local conditions. Ores and minerals, for example, can often be obtained in open-cast mines on or near the surface or alternatively have to be won from great depths through mining by way of shafts and tunnels; they occur in some locations in widely distributed lumps, in veins or galleries, in others in mighty, connected deposits, here almost in purity, elsewhere strewn into dead rock, difficult to extract, or they appear together with other chemicals in compounds. The variety of circumstances and conditions in nature of 'producing' 'goods' becomes apparent especially in the use of land for agriculture and other purposes because, depending on the way of utilizing it, depending on the composition of the soil, the climatic and economic predisposition of the land, very different rewards are reaped.

As with other enterprises, when obtaining produce from the land, the sum of the interest of the capital invested for the running of the business and of the running costs themselves must be kept to a minimum. Apart from the capital to be invested in buildings, equipment, machinery, animals etc., that is for the so-called inventory, capital to be invested for soil improvement must be considered when working the land – capital which is not to achieve a decrease in running costs but an increase in yields. Costs include expenditure for draining, irrigation and fertilizers. If the monetary return for the annual harvest on a land unit, the gross profit, equals E, if the running cost at a usefully measured level of the capital invested in the inventory, including interest, capital repayment and insurance of the inventory equals B for the land unit, and finally, the interest of the capital invested in soil improvement equals Ai, then the *net profit* equals $R = E - B - Ai$.

This net profit is at the same time the income derived from the land, that is that part of the gains from the land which remains after all expenses for the working of the land and improvements to the soil have been deducted. The income derived from the land is therefore dependent on the naturally existing conditions, on the prices of goods and labour and the careful planning with which the enterprise and soil improvement have been carried out, keeping in mind the prevailing interest rate.

The gross proceeds, E, of the land unit depend on the size of the capital, A, for soil improvements; it is some function, F(A), of A. The most favourably measured running costs B originating from expenditure for inventory, depend, even if only to a small extent, on the capital for soil improvement because they decrease per unit of produce relative to the running costs and the improvement of the soil, but they increase as a total amount for the total land under production. If therefore B = f(A), then the returns from the land are:

$$R = F(A) - f(A) - Ai.$$

The returns from land reach their highest level when:

$$F'(A) - f'(A) - i = 0. \tag{75}$$

Figure 10 shows the highest returns from land. The abscissae indicate the capital invested in soil improvement, the ordinates up to the rising line OA therefore show the interest of the capital invested in soil improvement, the spaces measured between the rising line OA and the curve BCD parallel to the ordinates show the running costs, B = f(A), and finally the ordinates of the curve EFG indicate the gross proceeds of the land. The spaces between the lines indicating the running costs BCD, and the proceeds EFG give the net profit or proceeds from the land which reaches its highest level, FC, at an investment in soil improvement capital, OH.

If the returns from land are divided by the interest rate, the capital value of the block of land can be determined. The owner of a block of land gains only that part of the proceeds of his holdings as profit by which this exceeds the interest on the price paid for the purchase of the block of land.

The costs invested in the soil improvement are usually only partly known so that the proceeds from the land still contain the expenditure for soil improvement which have remained unknown, and therefore the *net* proceeds from the land which are part of the

Figure 10

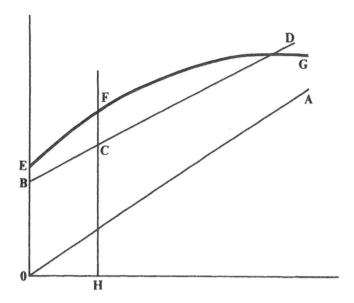

circumstances given in nature and the economic situation, are mostly much lower than the calculated amount. But the net proceeds from land-holdings are only considered in the context of scientific investigation; they are without practical meaning.

The proceeds from land change with prices obtained for produce, wages and interest rates; they rise with growing prices for *procedure* and raw materials and with a drop in wages and interest rates. The price of produce depends on the demand which exists for the individual goods and on the supply of these, that is on the size of the land which is being cultivated. If the suitable block of land were infinite in its size then the area of cultivation would be extended to such a degree that the produce could be sold only at a price which would cover merely the running costs for the poorest and most distant of all the blocks of land. With the extension of the area under cultivation, the price for the produce will decrease and with it the level of proceeds for *all* blocks of land, until the proceeds for the poorest and most distant block of land of the total area under cultivation has become zero. Therefore the returns from land-holdings represent a perceived calculation of the advantages which the better blocks of land have over the last block, which is only just worth the effort of working it.

If it is impossible to extend the arable land area to that borderline where the returns from the land for the poorest block become zero, then the returns of *all* blocks remain higher. *The level of returns from the land depends on the productivity of the total area of arable land available for the provision of food supplies for a given population.*

The demand for a certain type of produce with a utility function of $\alpha x - \alpha_1 x^2$ amounts, according to equation (63), to:

$$N = nw(\alpha/w - p)/2\alpha_1.$$

If a surface area of b is available to cover this demand, and supplies a return of γ units of goods, then the following equation arises:

$$\gamma b = nw(\alpha/w - p)/2\alpha_1$$

hence:

$$p = \alpha/w - 2\alpha_1\gamma b/nw.$$

If the running costs, including interest for the equipment and machinery and for the capital invested in soil improvement, amount to p^0 per unit, then the proceeds from the land are $r = (p - p^0)\gamma$ or:

$$r = \gamma(\alpha/w - p_0 - 2\alpha_1\gamma b/nw). \tag{76}$$

The proceeds from the land therefore increase with the increase in population n/b and its affluence. However it will reach a maximum for a certain productivity of the soil, given by:

$$\gamma = nw(\alpha/w - p_0)/4\alpha_1 b. \tag{77}$$

The result, expressed in (75) that *at a given population density the proceeds from the land for a certain productivity of the soil reaches its highest level*, is clear because at low productivity of the soil the price per unit of produce will be high, but the yield per unit of land will remain low due to the small number of harvested units; in contrast, if the soil gives a high yield, the price per unit of produce will be low and will amount in spite of the high yield to a low total income for the size of the land. This remains true only as long as the price for produce stays within the price range existing between import and export prices (cf. Chapter 31).

Returns from land-holdings do not only develop from agricultural use of the land or by building developments, but also from other usage depending on particular characteristics of the soil and tied to certain locations, as for example from the cutting of peat, clay, sand, lime, rocks and minerals of many kinds. Utilization of other local conditions and natural forces, as for instance a small waterfall, come under the heading of net profit returns from land holdings.

Any local advantages, for example a bay suitable for a harbour, a beach suitable for swimming, a sandbank suitable for the growing of oysters, a stream useful for fishing or a place with scenic views, provide for the locality potential returns from land-holdings. Just like these natural circumstances, man-made installations like roads, railways and canals as well as human settlements influence the level of value of land-holdings. Finally, improvements in technical enterprises of using the land often decidedly improve the land value and its returns.

It will be realized from all this that the returns from land depend on many circumstances and are subject to variations, and especially that *they should not be looked upon as a gift from nature to man but they merely represent an estimate of the advantages which a block of land possesses in relation to a particular way of utilizing it,* regardless of whether these advantages find their origin in nature or were established by human labour.

24. The Interest Rate

It was proved in Chapter 15, by establishing the basic rule for the formation of capital, to what extent the supply of newly established capital investments depends on the offered interest rate. Demand versus supply is composed of the following amounts:

1. Capital investment which is necessary to maintain the existing capital assets. This is the expenditure for maintenance of all kinds of buildings, machinery, tools, furniture and equipment, clothing etc.
2. Capital for replacement of existing assets. This must be interpreted as being calculated on the basis of the annual repayment which in business language is described as depreciation. The repayments will have to accumulate with interest and compound interest to that date when the necessary replacement will take place up to the level of capital necessary for the replacement purchase.
3. Capital for the replacement of assets accidentally destroyed. In many cases the place of this capital is taken by insurance premiums.
4. Capital for the implementation of improvements and completions of a production or manufacturing plant. The costs arising from soil improvements by drainage, irrigation, fertilization etc., the expenditure for improvement of public transport and roads and all costs arising from the implementation of new processes and inventions belong into this category.
5. Capital for the construction of new plants and factories becoming necessary due to increased demand for consumer goods because of growing affluence or an increase in population.
6. Capital spent carelessly by a wasteful lifestyle.

The demand for capital arising from the above listed causes depends in its extent on the prevailing interest rate, but this dependence is not demonstrated in the same way for every cause cited above. The

122

repayment rates in the second group are calculated at an interest i when the replacement capital A must be available in n years, according to Chapter 21, at an annual amount, $t = Ai/\{(1+i)^n - 1\}$. The annual repayment of the capital will be larger, the lower is the interest rate.

The same calculation and therefore the same dependence of the capital supply is arrived at for the third group of capital demand which arises from replacement of assets destroyed by accident. The annual insurance rate must be calculated on the basis of the probability of loss through accident and accordingly the figure n must be added to the formula.

The costs listed in the first group for the maintenance of assets will, if calculated generously, extend the duration of the capital so that an increase in the maintenance costs will lower the repayment instalments. Maintenance costs must therefore be calculated in such a way that the sum of annual maintenance expenditure and of repayments remains relatively small. Again, out of this demand arises the need for a calculation of maintenance costs at a level proportionally higher, the lower the interest rate is because the repayments, growing with a lowering of the interest rate, demand decidedly more careful maintenance provisions through which the period of repayment will become longer.

The interdependence of interest rates and the demand for capital by the fourth and fifth group listed is demonstrated clearly in equation (70) applicable to a production factory as developed in Chapter 21, according to which the first derivative in the running costs equation must be equal to the interest rate, and is demonstrated also in equation (75), Chapter 21, referring to the capital intended for soil improvement. Finally, the capital mentioned in the sixth group of capital demand will be increasingly needed with a decrease in the interest rate, as becomes apparent without doubt in the discussions of Chapter 15.

The equating of all capital demands, expressed in terms of their dependence on the prevailing interest rates, with the total supply of capital arising from the basic equation of the formation of capital in Chapter 15, determines the level of interest rates:

$$\frac{i}{i_0} = \frac{F'(e-x)}{F'(e+ix)}.$$

A small decrease in interest rates raises the demand for capital considerably, and at the same time the supply of capital decreases to a considerable extent, so the fluctuation of rates of interest must be confined within narrow borders. The prevailing interest rate i will always have to remain higher, but must be only very slightly higher than the rate i_0 which is demanded by savers. The interest rate which is being demanded is based on an estimate of the minimum value which a future pleasure has compared to an equally great pleasure available in the present. This estimate of value must vary from one person to another depending on the individual's philosophy of life, but will vary for the majority, independent of individual views, in the cause of historic developments. In times of general insecurity when nobody knows what tomorrow may bring, where fear surpasses hope for the future, future pleasures will be valued less compared to pleasures of the present, therefore the demanded interest rate, the 'fee', for waiting for future pleasures or the compensation for a delayed pleasure, will be set at a high level. In this way, sometimes a whole nation, or even a whole era, is drawn into a frenzy of *'après nous le déluge'*. In such times the demand for capital is small for two reasons, not only because of the high interest rate, but also because courage to start new ventures is lacking and maintenance of existing facilities will be reduced to a minimum. In this situation the prevailing interest rate will be raised only minimally above the demanded level, but due to the level of the latter, will still be high.

If however, in a contrary situation, peace and order are seen to be secured for a long time to come, then the pleasure envisaged in the future will not be estimated to be of a much lower value than the presently available one; a lower level of interest will be demanded, a smaller compensation for waiting for future pleasure. The entice-ment to start new ventures will however be raised considerably through the feeling of lasting security, the demand for capital will be very considerable, due to which a rise in interest rates will be caused by the supply created to satisfy this demand.

The opposite causes therefore lead in both cases to the same result of high interest rates. On the one hand, despair about the future leads to consumption, as long as there is still time, and therefore to a high estimate of the demanded interest rate so that the prevailing interest rate is high although it lies only marginally above the demanded one; on the other hand, safe hope leads to wise consider-ation of the future, so that the demanded interest rate will be at a low level, but the prevailing interest rate will rise due to a considerably higher level of a lively spirit of enterprise.

A lowering of the prevailing interest rate will not occur until confidence in the future remains, while saturation level or even over-saturation of the entrepreneurial market has been reached. In such times an increase in the level of interest rates can only be expected when forecasts of future developments become more pessimistic.

Finally it should be pointed out that the level of the demanded interest rate depends also on the degree of security which can be provided by the borrower. This aspect will not have any bearing, however, on the determination of the level of the interest rate derived from the balance of demand and supply because the increase in the interest rate for unsecured borrowing compared to the normal rate is due only to the added costs for insurance against possible loss.

25. Wages and Salaries

The level of wages and salaries is determined in a very similar way to that in which income from land and company profits are determined. Assume given utility functions of certain goods as well as a number of persons and their affluence who, in relation to their income, demand these goods. To satisfy, at a given price, the level of demand, the labour of a number of workers, as determined in equations (64) and (65) of Chapter 20, is necessary whose rate of pay is initially arbitrarily determined by the given price of the goods.

If the production of all consumer goods were organized in this manner, then the wages of the workers employed in the various production plants and factories would vary greatly, together with the arbitrarily determined prices of goods. The consequence of this would be that a large surge of workers would take place to those places where large rewards are achieved. Sales of the increased production in these enterprises could only be achieved by a lowering of prices which would be followed by a lowering of wages. This decrease in prices of goods and wages would be perpetuated until the rate of pay reached such a level that no additional workers would be attracted. The workers turning to better paid jobs would be drawn from poorly paying employers who, no longer able to satisfy demand, would have to increase wages and prices of goods.

If all jobs were equally demanding and all workers equally capable, then the movement of the workforce would only settle after the prices of goods were regulated in such a way that all employers paid equal wages. If, after this balance is reached, unemployed workers still existed, these would then offer their work at a slightly lower rate of pay, which would cause a lowering of the uniform level of wages and all prices of goods, to that level at which all workers have found employment, or until the emergency rate of pay has been reached at which the unemployed will no longer attempt to find employment because the toil of labour equals the level of 'enjoyment of life' obtainable through wages.

The claim expressed in the establishment of the *iron rule of wages* and according to which wages must drop to the emergency rate of pay, cannot be proved and is patently wrong. The rates of pay and surplus of pleasure over the drudgery of labour achievable through these rates of pay depend on the generally advancing development of human activity.

It is not of course the absolute level of the rate of pay that is decisive, but its ratio in comparison to the prices of consumer goods. If the rate of pay were doubled then, after overcoming every temporary disruption due to changes and all obstacles, prices of all goods would have to double, so that the level of pleasure obtainable through wages would remain unchanged. As the costs of preparatory and productive work would double due to the doubling of the rate of pay, double the investment capital would become necessary for the establishment of a new enterprise. Existing employers could then determine the price of goods, without the threat of competition from new enterprises, as if their investment capital had doubled. Their capital as well as their profit will reach double the level so that the income of all persons – workers, capital investors and managers – will double, thus doubling the amount disposable for the purchase of an unchanged quantity of goods, which will be followed by a doubling of the price of goods. The income from capital, nevertheless, is now divided differently among individual persons in that the increase in the capital value does not benefit the proprietors of the capital who have lent the capital, but the managers who utilize the capital, because the interest rate remains unchanged by these price changes as every demand for capital which will always be used for the payment of wages, and every supply of capital which depends on the income and the costs needed for complete saturation, will have to double.

A general increase in wages cannot therefore increase the reward for workers, merely the persons living off the interest from investment capital compared to those in possession of the invested capital; that is, the capital investor compared to the landowner and producer of any kind will suffer. But an increase in wages benefiting a limited number of workers will better their lot at the expense of the rest of humanity.

A uniform rate of pay will not occur, due to the great variety of chores to be performed and the great variety in the ability of workers. Only the most capable workers will be able to compete for the most demanding jobs, workers who, as well as being naturally talented, were able to invest the necessary capital in a satisfactory education. With an increased influx of suitable workers to these most difficult job areas, it will become clear without further explanation that the rate of pay will drop until the level has been reached at which workers will no longer be attracted.

Not everyone who chooses the same occupation will reach the same level of satisfaction, because the output of work will vary according to diligence and dexterity and with it the rate of pay, as will the estimate of the toil factor, and accordingly the level of pleasure surplus will vary even at the same rate of pay. The professions of architect, solicitor, doctor sometimes do not even allow those who do not have the talent, who are not sufficiently diligent, or lack the ability to present themselves favourably, to recover the capital invested in their education. This happens more frequently when more-qualified persons seek employment or work in those overly popular professions and thus effect a movement of the less-suitable ones to other professions. In this way, many of them will see themselves pushed step by step lower and lower, giving way to those more talented and more favoured, until those with the least personal advantages and the smallest capital will have to turn to those jobs which demand the lowest level of intelligence and physical ability or dexterity and the lowest level of education. For each of the levels of performance the level of pay will be determined according to the rules developed in Chapter 20 depending on the extent of demand and the number of workers offering their services. A strong supply of labour will lower wages and push a section of the workforce down to a lower level of work. The lesser-performing workers obtain a lower level of pleasure surplus in a higher-level position than the better-performing workers in a lesser job. The rate of pay on the lowest level of labour has to be small because a small increase of the rate would already suffice to attract a number of workers from higher positions who occupy the lower rungs on that level which would once again depress the rate of pay. On the lowest job level which requires neither physical strength nor education the weakest workers will be unable to obtain anything but the emergency rate of pay.

Dependent on the level of initial talents and the capital invested in education, the same rules apply to the gradation of wages as to the returns from land-holdings and company profit. Just as the income from a block of land situated in the poorest and least-suitable position will cover only running costs, that it does not provide a profit, and the weakest manufacturer only earns enough through the sales of his products to cover his own labour, in the same way the weakest and least-able worker will, with his wages only cover the bare minimum cost of living without reaching a pleasure surplus over the toil of work. But just as soil of excellent composition on the sunny side of a hill and in the best economic position, after suitable drainage, irrigation, and application of fertilizer, will give high returns, and just as the component and diligent manager after working out the best way of investing capital will obtain a large profit, in the same way the capable worker, after a correct estimate of the capital to be invested in his education, will receive high wages for his labour. Just as returns from land and company profits increase due to the growing affluence of the community and the growing demand for consumer goods that follows this, so wages will also increase.

However, one important difference between company profits on the one hand and returns from property holdings and wages and salaries on the other must not be disregarded. There will never be a lack of businessmen in any economic society, so the push of additional businessmen will end only when, for the weakest of them, the profit is zero. In contrast there will always be a limit to arable land so that even for the poorest block of land being cultivated the income will not amount to zero. Equally the number of persons offering their labour will not always be unlimited or larger than the number of workers needed so that the lowest rate of pay will not always reach the level of the emergency rate of pay.

There can never be a lack of sick or malingering persons who cannot reach the emergency rate of pay and therefore do not work at all because the toil of labour which would ensure a minimal living for them would be perceived by them as so heavy that they could not make the effort in order to achieve mere survival; these persons will be supported by social services or end up in work camps.

Unfortunately, it is also an undisputable fact that in times of economic disaster not all who seek work will find it, a situation which led to the concept of 'the right to work'. This problem cannot be solved by economic means, but only by applying principles of human charity. It is not a question of a *right existing for those suffering deprivation* but instead a *duty to act* of those who can help, just as someone drowning does not have the right to be saved from death, but someone who is able to assist has the duty to pull him on to dry land. Nobody will dispute that in a case where the power or the charity of individuals does not suffice to bring about improvement, human society, be it the small community or the state, must come to the rescue. By way of suitable economic institutions like the Social Security Department mentioned earlier, who keep themselves continuously informed about the state of the labour market and can give reliable information about it, perhaps by way of insurance, considerable easing of the discussed state of crisis can be effected.

After the demonstration given above of the processes in accordance with which rates of pay are regulated, the term *natural wages* as von Thünen tries to develop it in his work *The Isolated State* (3rd edn, Part 2, p. 150) can no longer be maintained. It is easy to prove the error in von Thünen's conclusion which is an example of the erroneous application of mathematics to economic problems, by which the application of mathematics to the solution of economic problems has come into disrepute.

Von Thünen equates the emergency rate of pay at which the worker can just survive and maintain himself in a state of being able to work to a, but the wages that he should receive to a + y. If a worker supplies in the course of a day a work performance to the value of p then a surplus of p − a − y will have been achieved by him, that is, if a number of workers n is employed in a company, the total surplus for the company will be n(p − a − y). If, for the establishment of the company, preparatory work of nq working days was necessary, then prior to the commencement of production in the plant, wages equalling nqa would have had to be paid to the workers employed to assure the payment of the minimum survival wage. Von Thünen supposes that for the provision of these minimum survival wages for the workers employed in the establishment, a second group of workers paid at a rate of a + y works, but that these workers are content with the emergency pay rate, a giving away the surplus, y, to enable the first group of workers to establish the plant. This second group of workers must work nqa/y working days so that both groups work nq + nqa/y = nq(y + a)/n working days to establish the plant and are satisfied during this period of time with receiving the emergency rate of pay, a. For this sacrifice the workers are now supposed to receive the company profit which amounts to

$$\frac{n(p-a-y)}{nq(y+a)/y} = \frac{(p-a-y)y}{q(y+a)}$$

for each day spent on the preparatory work. This surplus will become a maximum for $a + y = \sqrt{ap}$. The figure $\sqrt{ap}$ is thereafter called the natural rate of pay by von Thünen.

The error of this interpretation lies in the fact that the level of deprivation which is accepted by the workers employed in the establishment of the plant, by being content with the emergency rate of pay, must not be measured according to the number of days during which they endured the deprivation, but according to the extent of this deprivation which amounts to y for each day. The figure for the deprivation is therefore nq $(a + y)$; if the company profit is divided by this, then the result arrived at is $\{1/(a+y) - 1\}/q$, a figure which is largest when $y = 0$. This cannot be different when the question of the rate of pay is viewed from the position of the employer, as the company profit will be the larger, the lower is the rate of pay.

26. Money and the Formation of Prices

It has been supposed, because of an erroneous interpretation of the role played by money in the economy, that due to a growth in money available, its value would be diminished and therefore prices of goods would rise, and the blame for actual increases in all prices has been put on an increased output of coinage by the mint, but mainly to the mass printing of paper money and the increased use of drafts and financial paper values of a similar kind.

The surest way of arriving at the proper insight into the effects of money is to look at a smaller, self-contained economic community. Imagine that a small producer has arranged for the workers paid by him to do all their shopping at sources which are administered by his business interests, as practised for example in the large enterprise of Krupp in Essen, to a large extent to supply workers with high-quality, low-priced goods. If all of the workers' needs are cared for in this manner, then their wages will be returned by the end of the pay period of one week almost entirely to the cash register of the company, so that the money circulating continuously in this economic community will not exceed by much the amount of the weekly wages. But if the payment of wages did not occur on a weekly basis but in periods of a fortnight or four weeks, then nearly double or four times the amount of circulating money would be necessary without the prices of labour or goods having to experience the slightest variation. *The quantity of money necessary for circulation depends on the velocity of circulation and has no bearing on prices.*

If workers in the enterprise under discussion receive a one-off double payment of wages, but the rate of pay remaining for the rest unchanged, then the increased amount received would flow back into the company's cash register before long and the quantity of money circulating would soon be reduced to the old amount of the single week's wages. *The quantity of money in circulation cannot be increased above the level deriving from incomes and velocity of circulation.*

132

If the quantity of money is increased above this level in a state, perhaps through an additional issue of paper notes, then the surplus will come to rest somewhere, similar to water dripping from a saturated sponge. In economically well-developed circumstances everyone will avoid the collection of useless, idle money and push along the surplus until it comes to rest in the banks whose circulation of notes will experience a corresponding drop relative to the surplus of money. The banks will attempt to buy into foreign ventures to find room for their notes in the local money market and thus cause the transfer of precious metals to foreign countries to be replaced by bank notes in the local market. Restraint in the issue of government notes assists in the issue of notes by banks and keeps precious metals in the country. If a shortage of money is experienced in a state, supplementation is sought either through borrowing in foreign countries or by issuing artificial means of payment like drafts, letters of credit etc.

For economic intercourse a certain quantity of money, be it metal coinage, paper money or any other kinds of papers used for payment, is needed which cannot continuously be varied, but the fluctuations of which are evened out from time to time by increasing or decreasing the circulation of drafts and bank notes. *The quantity of money does not influence the prices of goods and labour. Prices are determined by the sum of the income of all individuals.*

It was proved in Chapter 15 what part of an income must be put aside as savings. The incentive to save is the greater, the higher is the prevailing interest rate and the higher are the pleasures of the future compared to those of the present. The remaining income will be used to pay for the goods consumed or utilized in accordance with the rules developed in Chapter 14 for the balance in the budget. Apart from a small remainder negligible in relation to the whole, use of all existing services and goods and the price for all consumer goods produced within a year are paid for from the yearly income of the total community.

Priceworthiness depends on the size of incomes of individuals up to which they can afford to buy so that the demand for a good with the utility function $\alpha x - \alpha_1 x^2$ amounts to $x = (\alpha - wp)/2\alpha_1$. If the total supply, a, of goods is to be exhausted by the total of n persons who are able to buy at an average priceworthiness, w, then the price p must be:

$$p = (\alpha - 2\alpha_1 a/n)/w.$$

As discussed in Chapter 22, the quantity, a, of the manufactured goods will regulate itself in such a way that the weakest producer engaged in production will just recover his costs. A price change will occur when the income changes on which the priceworthiness w to be achieved depends.

Just as income consists of wages, capital interest and company profit, so the price of goods pays for wages, capital interest and company profit. Every change in income changes the means available with which to pay for goods and the money spent on the production of goods at an equivalent rate. The increase or drop of prices developing in this way depends on which of the sources of income causes the rise or fall of income.

If e is the average income of persons, then according to equation (32) in Chapter 14 the priceworthiness at which purchases will be made, is:

$$\frac{\sum(\alpha p'/2\alpha_1 + \beta p''/2\beta_1 + \ldots) - e}{\sum(p'^2/2\alpha_1 + p''/2\beta_1 + \ldots)}.$$

If in accordance with the quantity of goods available a, b, c etc. these are distributed per person at a rate of $a/n = a_1$, $b/n = b_1$ then prices, from equation (31), Chapter 14, must amount to:

$$p' = (\alpha - 2\alpha_1 a_1)/w \tag{78}$$

$$p'' = (\beta - 2\beta_1 b_1)/w.$$

By substituting these values for the prices in the above equation, priceworthiness will amount to:

$$w = \sum \{a_1(\alpha - 2\alpha_1 a_1) + b_1(\beta - 2\beta_1 b_1) + \ldots\}/e \tag{79}$$

and substituting into (78), prices of goods will be:

$$p' = \frac{(\alpha - 2\alpha_1 a_1)e}{\sum\{a_1(\alpha - 2\alpha_1 a_1) + \ldots\}} \tag{80}$$

$$p'' = \frac{(\beta - 2\beta_1 b_1)e}{\sum\{a_1(\alpha - 2\alpha_1 a_1) + \ldots\}}$$

and so on.

In a case where the average quantity of goods per person remains unchanged, prices of all goods must always vary in proportion to the average income of all persons. The formation of prices therefore depends on the extent to which a change in income influences the quantity of goods produced, a fact which remains to be investigated separately for the various sources of income.

If for example half the sum of everybody's income consisted of capital interest, then, at a drop of the interest rate by one-tenth of its amount, the average income of all persons would be diminished by one-twentieth of its earlier amount and therefore the prices of all goods would drop by one-twentieth. An increased profit would arise for all goods, the price of which is more than half made up of capital interest, while in the opposite situation the company profit will be reduced for those goods where less than half the cost of production is contained in capital interest. For the latter goods there will be a reduction in the quantity produced, while for the goods in the first group an increase in production occurs. This is followed by a greater drop in prices for such capital-intensive goods than that for goods produced with only a small investment of capital. There will be no end to this movement of prices until the price of all goods has dropped to an amount equal to the savings which result from a drop in interest rates in the production costs. As the rate of pay is not affected by this price change, *all persons whose income consists of wages will gain by the drop in prices due to a drop in the interest rate.*

This fact will, however, be temporarily overturned because, in accordance with the rule in Chapter 21 governing the basic equation of a production plant, the producing labour will be reduced at the time of dropping interest rates with an increase in the investment capital, i.e. with increased preparatory work. The growth in investment capital will initially lead to increased labour activity which cannot come about without increases in wages. But this is only a passing phenomenon as, after the tying-down of the investment capital, the labour needed for production work will decrease and with it the level of wages. But the increased living standard enjoyed by workers will not suffer through this development because prices for goods will also decrease due to the decreased rates of pay. With an increase in the interest rate the opposite effect will develop; prices of goods will rise and workers will suffer a slump in their standard of living.

However, the influence with greater impact on the level of the average income than that of the relatively small movements of interest rates within their narrow boundary, is the steady growth of capital. If it is supposed for example that in an economic community where capital interest supplies half the total income, capital will slowly reach double its original amount, and the average income will increase to 1.5 times its former size; the increase in prices of goods caused by this circumstance must lead to increased production of goods which will depress prices of goods in turn while wages will slightly rise. The owners of capital whose income has doubled while prices of goods did not quite reach 1.5 times their former level, therefore gain considerably, while workers will not easily achieve an increase in wages which equals the increase in the prices of goods. Especially in times of rapid capital growth, workers will end up in a difficult situation.

Increased company profit will have the same effect as capital growth which in times of rapidly improving production methods, i.e. through inventions breaking new ground, will reach, if temporarily, extreme heights. It is of great importance, however, to remember that for the maintenance of former standards of living of workers, wages do not necessarily have to rise in the same proportion as capital growth and company profit. This can be explained by the fact that with an increase in income the increase in consumption is only partly directed towards former consumption goods, but to a larger extent towards luxury goods which were not previously used. The less-affluent consumer does not therefore experience considerable competition from the better-off for goods which are necessities. The prices of these cheaper goods do not experience, according to equation (80), any increase worth mentioning because the denominator, by including the new goods in the summation sign, grows almost to the same extent as does the average income. Nevertheless an increase in price for some goods will occur which will surpass the increase in wages so that with the growth in capital and company profit the workers' battle for wage increases is fully justifiable.

In discussing the growth of capital above, the capital referred to consists entirely of *physical assets*. Securities, shares, obligations and such are nothing but titles by which the size of the share in revenue or profit in enterprises is regulated. Someone who may have succeeded in obtaining all the shares of a production enterprise does not own anything but the proof of his ownership and can, as soon as his rights have been documented in another way, burn the shares without losing a cent. In a similar way, *money, too, is nothing but a tangible entitlement to a certain quantity of pleasure; it is not equal to goods which are usable or consumable but is only a representative symbol of both.*

PART 3

The Transport of Goods

27. Market Area for the Sale of Goods

The price at which goods leave the location of their origin usually experiences an additional charge for the cost of dispatching them from the location of origin to the location of use or consumption. Due to the increase in price relative to an increasing distance to be covered by transport, demand will decrease, and after a certain distance from the place of origin, deteriorate to zero.

If p is the price payable for goods at the place of origin and f the rate of freight for a given unit and size of goods, the price resulting at a distance, z, from the place of origin is $p + fz$. If then α is the marginal utility of the first unit for the consumer who can buy, in accordance with his financial status, at a priceworthiness of w, then the maximum dispatch distance, z', at which goods become so expensive that demand ceases is determined thus:

$$\alpha/(p + fz') = w$$

and the maximum dispatch distance arrived at:

$$z' = (\alpha/w - p)/f. \tag{81}$$

The goods can therefore bear the following additional dispatch expenses:

$$v = fz' = \alpha/w - p \tag{82}$$

which can be called the *dispatch value*. This is the amount by which the price p at the place of origin stays below the price α/w, for which the first unit is still purchased by the consumer who can buy, in accordance with his financial circumstances, at a priceworthiness of w.

The transport charges are estimated in proportion to the distance the goods will travel while – except for the 'differential tariffs' which are of no concern in this context – there are still regular additional costs irrespective of costs growing with the distance, which are independent of these, like packaging and loading, unpacking, storage and transport charges. Let us suppose that these charges which are independent of the distance have been included in the price p payable at the location of origin.

The goods will be sold everywhere within the maximum feasible distance, within the *dispatch borders*, so that the *market area* for a good which can be produced in a given location in unlimited quantity will form a circle, given that the respective economic conditions are equal in all directions, with a radius which equals the furthest dispatch distance. In the opposite direction, a location of consumption of goods, which depends on the expanse of the land, can be supplied from the total area right up to the dispatch borders. The area thus determined by both an area of selling and of buying is its *market area*.

When investigating the economic conditions in a market area one must differentiate strictly whether the area under investigation is for the sale of goods which can be produced in a single spot in any quantity regardless of the expanse of land around, as occurs in mining or mass production or the import business, or whether one deals with an area to be supplied, in which the quantity of the produced goods depends on the expanse of the land, as with the supply, to an area of consumption or a place of export, of agricultural produce and products of the timber industry.

Goods produced in a certain location have, depending on their value and weight, market areas of different sizes. The size of the market area is

$$\pi z'^2 = (\pi/f^2)(\alpha/w - p)^2$$

and under otherwise equal conditions is inversely proportional to the square of the freight rate.

If the utility function is based once more on the previously used formula $\alpha x - \alpha_1 x^2$, which can be supposed to be approximately correct, then for a consumer who can purchase at a priceworthiness of w, demand at a price of $p + fz$ becomes:

$$x = \{\alpha - (p+fz)w\}/2\alpha_1.$$

If the buyers are evenly distributed over the market area so that there are n buyers per surface unit, then total sales within the market area are:

$$\frac{n\pi}{\alpha_1} \int_0^{z'} \{\alpha - (p+fz)w\}\, z\, dz$$

that is:

$$\frac{n\pi}{\alpha_1} \{(\alpha - pw)z'^2/2 - fwz'^3/3\}$$

or, because the longest dispatch distance is $z' = (\alpha/w - p)/f$, or with the introduction of the dispatch value $v = \alpha/w - p$, amounts to $z' = v/f$ it follows that

$$Q = \frac{n\pi w v^3}{6\alpha_1 f^2}. \tag{83}$$

Sales therefore increase in proportion to the cube of the dispatch value and inversely in proportion to the square of the freight rate.

The weight to be transported per unit distance (ton kilometres) is:

$$V = \frac{n\pi}{\alpha_1} \int_0^{z'} \{\alpha - (p+fz)w\} z^2 dz$$

that is:

$$\frac{n\pi w v^4}{12\alpha_1 f^3}. \tag{84}$$

The number of transport units (ton kilometres) to be covered within a market area increases in proportion to the fourth power of the dispatch value and inversely in proportion to the cube of the freight rate.

The last two formulae demonstrate the extraordinary influence of improvement in the means of transport to the expansion of transport. Due to the building of roads, through which the freight rate compared to that on unmade roads was reduced to a third (from 75 pfennigs per ton kilometre to 25 pfennigs), the number of ton kilometres travelled for the sale of goods increased 27 times; due to railways which charge one-sixth of road transport, or in the example of coal, only one-tenth, further increases the quantity of goods transported by 36, or 100 times, and an increase of ton kilometres of 216, and even up to 1000 times had to occur.

The average dispatch distance of goods in the dispatch area is $z'' = V/Q = v/2f$, that is equal to half the furthest dispatch distance. The average price of goods corresponding to this average dispatch distance is:

$$p' = p + z''f = p + v/2$$

or, as $v = \alpha/w - p$,

$$p' = (\alpha/w + p)/2. \tag{85}$$

This means: *The average price at which buyers within the total market area obtain goods depends on the freight rate and represents the arithmetic mean of the price paid at the place of origin and that paid on the furthest borderline of the market area.*

When adding a profit margin, g, to the production price, p, of goods, the furthest dispatch distance decreases to $(\alpha/w - p - g)/f$, the dispatch value decreases to $v - g$ and total turnover becomes:

$$Q = \frac{n\pi w(v-g)^3}{6\alpha_1 f^2}$$

at which a total profit will be obtained by the company of:

$$G = \frac{n\pi wg(v-g)^3}{6\alpha_1 f^2}. \tag{86}$$

If the same number N of buyers were settled in close proximity to the origin instead of being spread across the entire market area, the demand would be:

$$Q_0 = N\{\alpha - (p+g)w\}/2\alpha_1$$

or, as $N = n\pi z'^2 = n\pi(\alpha/w - p - g)^2/f^2$, it amounts to:

$$Q_0 = n\pi w(\alpha/w - p - g)^3/2\alpha_1 f^2$$

$$= n\pi w(v-g)^3/2\alpha_1 f^2$$

whereby a total profit is obtained of:

$$G_0 = n\pi wg(v-g)^3/2\alpha_1 f^2. \qquad (87)$$

If the buyers are settled in close proximity to the origin of the goods instead of being distributed over the market area then sales and profits will increase threefold.

The higher the profit margin per unit, the more sales will decrease. If a businessman can exploit the production of certain goods as a *monopoly* then he will determine the profit margin in such a way that his total profit will reach a maximum. This most favourable profit margin is arrived at for sales within the market area by differentiation of equation (86) with respect to g at:

$$g' = v/4$$

whereby the total profit will amount to:

$$9n\pi wv^4/512\alpha_1 f^2. \qquad (88)$$

The number of buyers in the market would be $N = 9n\pi v^2/16f^2$. If this number of buyers were settled in the market centre, then the demand would be:

$$Q_0 = N\{\alpha - (p+g)w\}/2\alpha_1$$

$$= 9n\pi v^2\{\alpha - (p+g)w\}/32\alpha_1 f^2$$

and the profit would be

$$G_0 = 9n\pi v^2 g\{\alpha - (p+g)w\}/32\alpha_1 f^2$$

which reaches a maximum for:

$$g'' = (\alpha/w - p)/2 = v/2$$

that is, a maximum profit of:

$$G'' = 9n\pi wv^4/128\alpha_1 f^2. \qquad (89)$$

In a business which is conducted as a monopoly, profit will quadruple provided buyers are not widely dispersed in a market, but are all settled at the location of origin of the goods.

In the case where buyers are all in the vicinity of production they will have to pay a price $p + g'' = (\alpha/w + p)/2$. If they were dispersed over a market area, they would have to pay on average half the maximum freight rate for the furthest distance, i.e. $3(\alpha/w - p)/8$ and a price of $p + g' = \alpha/4w + 3p/4$, i.e. in total an average of $5\alpha/8w + 3p/8$, that is $(\alpha/w - p)/8$ more than if they lived at the point of origin of the goods.

Even in a case where the production of goods can be exploited as a monopoly, buyers of the goods will benefit if they are concentrated at the place of origin of the goods.

The three last formulae are of far-reaching importance for the change occurring in the pattern of human settlement through the improvement of transport facilities, and discussion will return to this aspect later on.

If the quantity of goods produced cannot be increased to a level where it can satisfy the greater demand from a market area enlarged by improved transport facilities, then the profit margin will be raised until the market area shrinks to such an extent that the remaining demand can be satisfied. A profit surcharge g would necessitate a quantity of goods:

$$Q = n\pi w(v - g)^3/6\alpha_1 f^2$$

from which the profit margin is:

$$g = v - \left(\frac{6\alpha_1 f^2 Q}{n\pi w} \right)^{1/3}. \tag{90}$$

It is obvious that this profit margin will increase dramatically with a decrease in the freight rate. Finally, it should be pointed out that for perishable goods like fish, fruit, vegetables, and milk a shortening of the time necessary for transport has the same effect as a fall in the freight rate. Some of the goods in this category, such as oysters and fresh fish the quantity of which cannot infinitely be extended, had to experience a considerable price rise through improved transport facilities and thus give their producers a considerably higher profit.

28. Market Area in Competition with Foreign Goods

A market area can contract through goods entering it from an outside origin. If the place of origin B of a second kind of good is situated at distance h from the place of origin A, and if the prices per unit at their places of origin are p' and p", and the freight rates f' and f" then at a point E in Figure 11 which lies at a distance x from A and y from B, both quantities of goods will have equal prices for equal quantities if the condition is fulfilled:

$$p' + f'x = p'' + f''y. \tag{91}$$

The line which demonstrates this condition is generally a closed curve of the fourth degree which belongs to the family of ellipses and is called an ellipse *secundi generis*. The curve incorporates the market area of the lesser goods, that is the heavier ones.

Figure 11

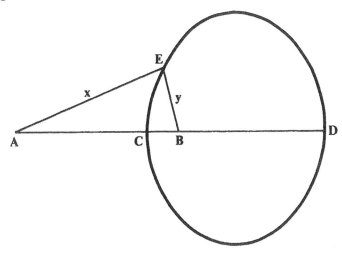

The smaller axis of the ellipse which lies in the direction of the line connecting the two places of origin has a length of:

$$CD = 2f''(p' - p'' + f'h)/(f''^2 - f'^2). \qquad (92)$$

In the case where $p' = p''$ the ellipse will change to a circle the centre of which does not, however, coincide with that of the place of origin.

If the goods produced in A and B are of equal value for equal weight quantities, i.e. if $f' = f''$, then the borderline of the market areas does not form a closed curve but changes to a hyperbola the hollow side of which is turned towards the more expensive place of origin. In the special case in which even the prices are equal at both places of origin, the hyperbola turns into a straight line cutting the connecting line of both locations to each other at a right angle.

The market area of a place of origin which is in competition with several other places all around will turn into a polygon the sides of which are formed by one of the just-mentioned conic section lines. The purchase areas to supply the neighbouring consumption places are delineated in the same manner.

The border between two market areas is situated on the line which measures h in length and which connects two neighbouring market places, distant from market place A by:

$$z' = (p'' - p' + f''h)/(f' + f''). \qquad (93)$$

The goods dispatched from B would be available in A at a price of $p'' + f''h$. The difference in price in A between the foreign and the local goods would therefore be $u' = p'' - p' + f''h$ (see Figure 12). By introducing this local price difference the following result is obtained:

$$z' = u'/(f' + f'') \qquad (94)$$

that is, with a drop in freight rates, the market area for the cheaper goods is expanded.

If the goods produced in A are the cheaper ones, they will, in the case that the freight rate f'' drops below the level of $f'' = (p'' - p')/h$, advance to the competitor's location of production.

If however the competing goods at a higher price are of better

Figure 12

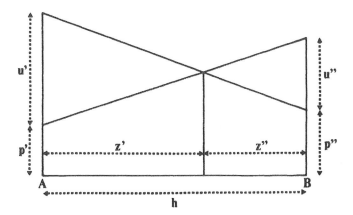

Figure 13

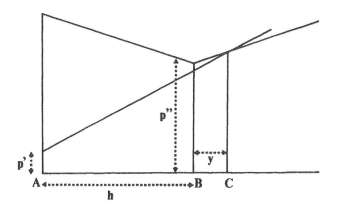

quality, meaning that at equal value they are lighter, so that f" is smaller than f', it will never be possible for the goods of lesser quality completely to displace these and retain their market share if elsewhere, when they have been displaced at their own place of origin by the goods of lesser quality. According to Figure 13, the price of goods A equals p' + f'h + f'y in the direction of BC, the price of goods B equals p" + f"y; thus goods B retain their market beyond C while it has been beaten at its place of origin, as soon as

$$y = (p'' - p' - f'h)/(f' - f''). \tag{95}$$

The improvement of the means of transport is dangerous to the more expensive goods: they lose the most effective of all protective tariffs, the protection through poor roads. But when the dearer goods are also the better-quality goods, they will never be completely displaced by the cheaper but lesser-quality goods, even if they are superseded at their own place of origin. But the cheaper goods are always advantaged by the improved transport conditions.

With less-developed transport facilities, even expensive goods of poor quality can dominate a market, while cheaper or better quality goods from a long distance cannot enter into competition with them. The improvement of the means of transport, which had a similar effect to that of the invention of gunpowder and the improvement of weapons, opened the possibilities for cheaper and better goods to take up the fight of competition from a greater distance. *Due to the perfection of the means of transport a mighty incentive has emerged which makes attempts and efforts plausible which aim at the reduction of prices for production and for improvements in the quality of goods.*

The increased importance which a low price for goods has with increasing improvements in the means of transport, also has a bearing on the calculation by the producer of the most favourable rate of profit, which must be reduced with the perfection of transport facilities.

The extent of the sale of goods Q depends on the rate of profit per unit g; that is, it must equal $F(g)$ so that the overall profit $G = gF(g)$ must be a maximum at:

$$g = -F(g)/F'(g). \tag{96}$$

This is the formula developed earlier in equation (71) of Chapter 22. For it to be possible to reach the conclusion that this most favourable overall profit for the businessman must decrease with the decrease in the freight rate, $F(g)$ must however be known.

Let us demonstrate in a simple case the correctness of this supposition. The task is to supply the line which connects the two places of production that are engaged in competition, with goods constant in their quantity for a certain length unit, for example, a road with the necessary quarried rock. If the consumption per unit length is γ, then according to equation (93) the following total profit will be obtained if for place of production A an overall profit of g′ and for B a profit of g″ is levelled:

$$G' = \gamma g'(p'' + g'' - p' - g' + f''h)/(f'' + f')$$

which will reach a maximum for:

$$g' = (p'' + g'' - p' + f''h)/2. \tag{97}$$

The more, therefore, the profit margin g″ in B is reduced, the more producer A must also reduce his overall profit margin. The total profit of producer B is:

$$G'' = g''(p' + g' - p'' - g'' + f'h)/(f' + f'')$$

which will reach a maximum for:

$$g'' = (p' + g' - p'' + f'h)/2 \tag{98}$$

therefore B is again dependent on the profit margin g′ of businessman A. From (97) and (98) the most favourable profit rates are:

$$g' = \{(p'' - p') + (2f'' + f')h\}/3$$

$$g'' = \{(p' - p'') + (2f' + f'')h\}/3. \tag{99}$$

These profit margins form the *peaceful basis* for the two producers in their competitive struggle. *Both the competitors would lose part of their total profit as soon as one went above or below the uniform profit margin while his opponent left his prices unaltered.*

A numerical example will serve to clarify this result. A road of 18 km is to be newly constructed from A to B. If in A limestone at a price of 5 Marks and in B basalt at a price of 8 Marks per cubic metre can be obtained, with freight costs of 1 Mark per cubic metre for a distance of 1 km on the line of the unmade road; if the demand is 1000 cubic metres per km, then, as both kinds of rock have the same value as a foundation, the values will be as follows: $p' = 5$; $p'' = 8$; $f' = f'' = 1.0$; $h = 18$ and therefore the most favourable profit margin for the owner of the limestone quarry is $g' = 19$, and for the owner of the basalt quarry is $g'' = 17$. The limestone would be supplied on a length of $z' = 9.5$, and the basalt on a length of $z'' = 8.5$.

But for the maintenance of the road 1 cubic metre of basalt equals the value of 3 cubic metres of limestone, and the freight rate on the completed road is 0.4 Marks per cubic metre and per kilometre. Therefore the value for equal quantities of limestone and basalt are: $p' = (3)(5) = 15$; $f' = (3)(0.4) = 1.2$; $p'' = 8$; $f'' = 0.4$; thus $g' = 9\frac{2}{3}$, and $g'' = 19.13$. Limestone is used on a length of $z' = 6.0$, and the basalt on a length of $z'' = 12.0$.

But for the covering layer in the new construction, conditions are again different. The relative value of the rocks is equal to that of the road maintenance so that 1 cubic metre of basalt is of equal value to that of 3 cubic metres of limestone; but the delivery is on unmade roads so that $f' = 3$ and $f'' = 1$ can be applied, whereby $g' = 27\frac{2}{3}g'' = 44\frac{1}{3}$ Marks, $z' = 6.9$ and $z'' = 11.1$ result.

It can be recognized from these calculations that, due to the reduction of the freight rate from 1 Mark to 0.4 Marks, the unit profit for 1 cubic metre of basalt drops from $44\frac{1}{3}$ Marks to 19.13 Marks and for 1 cubic metre of limestone from $9\frac{2}{9}$ Marks to $3\frac{2}{9}$ Marks.

The above example shows that in *competition with foreign goods, due to the perfection of the means of transport the most favourable profit margin for the businessman must be calculated at a lower level,* resulting for consumers in a further reduction of prices which had already been lowered due to decreased freight rates. *The producer of the goods gains according to (88), only by the perfection of transport facilities if the extension of the market areas due to those improvements is not diminished by competition with foreign goods.*

29. Market Area in Competition with Local Goods

If there are several producers in one place who produce goods for the same purposes of consumption, then the sale of the goods will have to be achieved in competition with the other producers: The goods produced by the individual businessmen will, even if they serve the same purposes, not be, as a rule, completely equal in value.

The unit prices for the various goods will be applied to equal quantities so that the freight rates for these equal quantities will be different, that is higher for the goods of poorer quality where the unit used as quantity of equal value is heavier than the goods of better quality.

Goods of poorer quality which have a higher price than the better goods are of course excluded from competition. Better goods cannot be sold at a higher price than the lesser goods at the place of origin itself, but they will succeed at a certain distance from the place of origin over the lesser goods because they can be dispatched at a lower cost than the lesser ones.

If the price of the better goods is p' with a freight rate of f' and the price of a comparable quantity of the lesser goods is p'' with a freight rate of f'' then the equation

$$p' + f'x = p'' + f''x$$

demonstrates that for a distance of dispatch

$$x = (p' - p'')/(f'' - f') \qquad (100)$$

both goods are priced the same. *The market area of the lesser goods forms a circle, that of the better goods forms a circular ring extending beyond the circle.*

If the profit margins added to the production prices are g' and g'' respectively, then the border between the market areas is distant from the place of origin by

$$x = (p' + g' - p'' - g'')(f'' - f').   \tag{101}$$

If the producer of the better goods, the goods sold in the outer ring area, increases the quantity of production, then sales can only be achieved by way of reducing the profit margin so that the market area will not only be extended in an outward direction, but also towards the centre of the circle at the expense of the lesser goods. The producer of the lesser goods can fend off a reduction of his market area only by reducing the price of his goods by almost the same level as his opponent. The producer of the better goods can therefore sell his increased output only by an extension of his market area in an outward direction. The market area of the opponent will be diminished only marginally, in as far as he can sell the unchanged quantity of goods due to an increase in demand following a decrease in price in a now smaller area. If, on the contrary, the producer of the lesser goods increases the quantity of goods produced by him he must, to achieve sales, reduce the price, which forces his opponent to carry out an almost equal reduction in his price to regain what has been lost on the inner borderline through an outward push of the outer borderline. In their competition both producers are dependent on the pricing structure which the opponent has to set up to assure the sale of the goods produced by him. In this battle, there exists a *basis of peace* on which each of the producers regulates the quantity of production and the price of goods in such a way that the opponent cannot increase his total profit either by way of a simultaneous increase in production and reduction of price to obtain sales, nor by way of reduced production and the increased prices.

To clarify these facts let us look once more at the earlier, simple example in order to avoid the otherwise very complicated calculations whereby this time, however, the places of origin of both kinds of goods are taken to be situated at the same endpoint of the line.

If at the final point of a road of 18 km length for the maintenance of the surface basalt at a price of 9 Marks and limestone at a price of 5 Marks can be obtained, if a cubic metre per 1 km distance costs 0.4 Marks in freight, if, finally, 3 cubic metres of limestone have an equal value to that of 1 cubic metre of basalt for the maintenance of the road, then for quantities of equal value, the prices amount to $p' = 15$, $p'' = 9$ and the freight rates $f' = 1.2$ and $f'' = 0.4$. With a profit margin of g' and g'' the profit of both quarry owners is:

$$G' = g'(p' + g' - p'' - g'')/(f'' - f')$$

$$G'' = g''\{h - (p' + g' - p'' - g'')/(f'' - f')\}$$

which will become a maximum for:

$$g' = (p'' + g'' - p')/2$$

$$g'' = (p' + g' - p'' - hf'' + hf')/2$$

from which:

$$g' = \{(p'' - p') + h(f' - f'')\}/3$$

$$g'' = \{(p' - p'') + 2h(f' - f'')\}/3.$$

Substituting the figures, these become $g' = 2.8$ and $g'' = 11.6$, whereby the limit of usage for limestone is 3.75 km distant from the place of quarrying, so that the profit of the owner of the limestone is $(2.8)(3.75) = 10.5$, and that of the owner of the basalt is $(11.6)(14.25) = 165.3$. The sum of the most favourable unit profits for both owners $g' + g''$ is always equal to the difference in freight for the total length of the stretch of road to be supplied, that is $(f' - f'')h$.

At a price $p' = p'' + (f' - f'')h$, that is $p' = 23.4$, a price of 7.8 Marks per cubic metre, limestone would be excluded from competition; the unit profit for basalt would amount to 14.4 and the total profit be $(18)(14.4) = 259.2$. The owner of the basalt would have been able to eliminate limestone earlier, at a lower price, from competition, if he had been satisfied with a profit margin of $p' - p''$, that is with $15 - 9 = 6$, but would have gained only $(6)(18) = 108$, while at prices on the 'peace basis' he would have obtained a profit of 165.3. *The motto of 'live and let live' applies fully in economic competition.* Basalt would remain excluded from competition if g'' becomes zero, which is $p'' = p' + 22(f' - f'')h = 43.8$. It can be seen from this simple example, when making comparisons with calculations in Chapter 28, how local competition is far more dangerous for the businessman than that originating from foreign sources.

The calculation of the prices on the 'peace basis' was as simple as possible, because the demand was a fixed quantity independent of price. As, however, the use of basalt or limestone is not limited to the maintenance of a given length of road but, depending on price, will reach over a more or less extended road system, the question of price formation in local competition needs to be investigated in general terms.

If in one place an arbitrary number of businesses exists which produce equally valuable goods and sell these at a market price of p' then, according to (83), the total turnover of these goods is

$$Q = \frac{n\pi w}{6\alpha_1 f^2} (\alpha/w - p)^3.$$

The individual producers manufacture the goods at different prices p', p'' etc, which means the profit on each unit amounts to $g' = p - p$, $g'', = p' - p''$ etc. If one of the manufacturers produces the m-th share of the total production and if his production price is p_m and his unit profit $g_m = p - p_m$ then his profit comes to:

$$G_m = \frac{n\pi w}{6\alpha_1 m f^2} (\alpha/w - p)^3 g_m. \tag{102}$$

By striving to increase this profit the producer is led to increase production, which can only be sold through lowered prices. If the quantity produced was Q_m at a market price of p then, with an increase of production by dQ, the market price p has to be lowered by dp so that the total profit will amount to:

$$G_m + dG = (Q_m + dQ)(g_m - dp)$$

i.e. an increase in profit due to $G_m = Q_m g_m$ of:

$$dG = dQ\, g_m - Q_m\, dp - dQ\, dp. \tag{103}$$

If the level of the prevailing market price p is to be in accordance with the 'peace basis', then the producer must not be able to obtain a rise in profit due to the increased production of goods and the price variation following it. This necessitates that $dG = 0$, i.e. through second-order terms:

$$dQ\, g_m = Q_m\, dp$$

$$g_m = Q_m \frac{dp}{dQ}. \tag{104}$$

This is once more the repeatedly found basic rule for the producer's profit. If the following is introduced:

$$Q_m = \frac{n\pi w}{6\alpha_1 mf^2} (a/w - p)^3$$

and

$$\frac{dQ}{dp} = \frac{n\pi w}{2\alpha_1 f^2} (\alpha/w - p)^2$$

the following results:

$$g_m = (\alpha/w - p)/3m.$$

But because $p_m + g_m = p$ it follows that $g_m = (\alpha w - p_m - g_m)/3m$, that is:

$$g_m = \frac{\alpha/m - p_m}{3m + 1}. \tag{105}$$

If it is remembered that the sum of the production price and the profit margin equal the market price, $p_m + g_m = p$, then the share in the total turnover obtainable by the producer at the price p_m can be deduced from (105):

$$\frac{1}{m} = \frac{3(p - p_m)}{\alpha w - p} \tag{106}$$

$$= \frac{3g_m}{\alpha/w - p}. \tag{107}$$

The sum of the shares of all producers is unity, so if the number of producers is N:

$$1 = \{3Np - 3\Sigma(p' + p'' + \dots)\}/(\alpha/w - p)$$

or, if the average production price for all producers, $\Sigma (p' + p'' + \dots)/N = p_0$, is used:

$$1 = 3N(p - p_0)/(\alpha/w - p)$$

from which the market price of the goods is:

$$p = \frac{\alpha/w + 3Np_0}{3N + 1}. \tag{108}$$

Accordingly the unit profit of $g_m = p - p_m$ for each individual producer is:

$$g_m = \{\alpha/w - p_m + 3N(p_0 - p_m)\}/(3N + 1). \tag{109}$$

If the price of (108) is substituted into equation (106), the market share of the producer manufacturing the goods at a price of p_m in the total turnover is obtained as:

$$\frac{1}{m} = \frac{\alpha/w - p_m + 3N(p_0 - p_m)}{N(\alpha/w - p_0)}. \tag{110}$$

This is zero if the manufacturing price becomes:

$$p_m = (\alpha/w + 3Np_0)/(3N + 1)$$

which is equal to the market price given in equation 108. This last equation can alternatively be written:

$$p_m = p_0 + (\alpha/w - p_0)/(3N + 1). \tag{111}$$

This means, *goods are excluded from competition as soon as their production price exceeds the average production price of goods with which they are in competition, by more than the part of the average dispatch value of the goods.*

For the 'peace basis', according to (106) and (107), the quantity of goods with which each producer can participate in the production of goods is dependent on the price at which he produces the goods and on the profit margin which he reaches. The total profit obtained by the producer is $G_m = Q \, g_m/m$, that is after introducing the value of $1/m$ of equation (107):

$$G_m = 3Qg_m^2/(\alpha/w - p). \tag{112}$$

The total profit of each producer is therefore proportional to the square of the profit margin obtained by him.

If for example the highest price α/w at which certain goods can still be sold equals 12.5, if five producers exist who sell the goods at prices of 4; 4.25; 4.5; 4.75 and 5 so that the average price $p_0 = 4.5$, then, from (108) the market price must be:

$$p = \{12.5 + (3)(5)(4.5)\}/\{(3)(5) + 1\} = 5.$$

The producer with the highest price who produces the goods at the price of 5 would therefore, from (111), be excluded from the market. The producer with the lowest price would achieve, according to (106), a market share of

$$\frac{1}{m} = \frac{3(5 - 4)}{12.5 - 5} = \frac{2}{5}.$$

The remaining shares in order are 3/10, 2/10 and 1/10. The total profits of these four manufacturers would be in the proportions 16:9:4:1.

In the special case where all N producers supply the goods at the same price of p_0 this price would be:

$$p = g + p_0 = (\alpha/w + 3Np_0)/(3N + 1)$$

resulting in an equal profit margin for all producers of:

$$g = (\alpha/w - p_0)/(3N + 1). \tag{113}$$

The total turnover, after introducing the market price, p, of (108), becomes:

$$Q = \frac{9n\pi w}{2\alpha_1 f^2} \left\{ \frac{N(\alpha/w - p)}{(3N + 1)} \right\}. \tag{114}$$

If in (112) the values for p, Q and g of (108), (114) and (113) are introduced, then for each of the N producers, a total profit is obtained:

$$G_m = \frac{9n\pi w}{2\alpha_1 f^2} \left\{ \frac{N^2(\alpha/w - p_0)^4}{(3N + 1)} \right\}. \tag{115}$$

Equations (113), (114) and (115) demonstrate that *through the participation of a greater number of producers, the profit margin obtainable per unit as well as the total profit obtained by the individual producers is reduced, but the turnover of goods increases with the reduction in the price of goods.*

If the profit per unit, the total profit and the turnover achievable by the individual producer is put at 1, then for two producers the profit per unit amounts to 0.57, the total profit to 0.42 and the quantity of turnover to 1.49; in the case of three producers the profit per unit amounts to 0.4, the total profit to 0.23 and the quantity of turnover to 1.73; finally for ten producers the profit per unit comes to 0.13, the total profit to 0.028 and the quantity turned over to 2.15.

The impact of several producers participating in the production of goods will not manifest itself to the same extent as demonstrated in the example calculated here because the production price p_0 does not, as assumed here, remain the same when the total production of goods increases, and at the same time the quantity produced by a manufacturer decreases, because with an increase in total production, wages must rise, and with a decrease in production by the individual manufacturer the share of general expenditure in the price per unit increases considerably. If it were possible to express in a mathematical formula the dependence of the production price p_0 on the number of producers, then the number N of producers could be determined for whom the price of goods becomes lowest. If p_0 is equal to $f(N)$, then according to (113) the price of goods is:

$$p = g + p_0 = \{\alpha/w + 3Nf(N)\}/(3N + 1)$$

which becomes a minimum when the following equation is fulfilled:

$$N(3N + 1)\,f'(N) + f(N) = \alpha/w. \qquad (116)$$

This equation demonstrates that the economically most favourable number of producers participating in manufacture, that is the answer to the question of whether the production of goods must tend towards large or small manufacturing plants, depends on the formula $f(N)$ and on the value attached to the produced goods.

30. Market Area for Supply of Goods

If γ units of a good can be harvested per unit of land, then a circular area of radius, z', will supply a quantity, $\gamma\pi z'^2$. If no obstacles to an extension of the area of supply exist, it will be extended until landowners on the border of the market area can recover only the production costs p_0 of the goods; as long as a profit can be achieved the incentive for an extension of the area of cultivation will remain. In an unlimited market area the price, with a freight rate f, will thus be $p = p_0 + fz'$. The larger the market area grows, the more supply will increase, but the higher the price will become, too, and therefore the lower the demand. For a certain size of supply area, supply and demand will correspond to each other.

If the utility function is based on the formula $\alpha x - \alpha_1 x^2$ then for n consumers who can purchase at an average priceworthiness, w, total demand will be $nw(\alpha/w - p_0 - fz')/2\alpha_1$. If this is equal to the supply $\gamma\pi z'^2$, then:

$$z' = \frac{nwf}{4\alpha_1\gamma\pi}\left[\left\{\frac{8\alpha_1\gamma\pi}{nwf^2}(\alpha/w - p_0) + 1\right\}^{0.5} - 1\right]. \qquad (117)$$

The landowner situated at the outer margin of the market obtains merely the cost of production; he does not achieve any profit from cultivating his land so that the returns from the land equal zero. The owner settled closer to the market centre, at a distance z, receives the same market price for his produce $p = p_0 + fz'$ but needs to pay only fz for freight, profiting by $f(z' - z)$ per unit, that is $\gamma f(z' - z)$ for the block of land.

If for instance the population of a market is 50,000, the average priceworthiness at which they can purchase is 0.5, the quantity harvested per square kilometre, γ, is 4000, the freight rate $f = 1/50$, the production price $p_0 = 4$, and finally $\alpha_1 = 1/1000$ and $\alpha = 10$, then $z' = 39$, and $p = 4 + 39\ 150 = 4.78$, and the proceeds from

161

land in the immediate vicinity of the market place equals (4000) 39/
150 = 3120. If the population of the market were double, at
100,000, then $z' = 54.5$; the market price would rise to 5.09 and the
proceeds from the land in the immediate vicinity of the market place
to 4360. *With an increase in population the price of produce increases,
and so do the proceeds from land, though at a much slower rate than
the increase in population.*

If the freight rate is reduced from 1/50 to 1/250, a drop corresponding approximately to a replacement of roads by railways, then
the market area will expand from $z' = 39.0$ to $z' = 39.9$; the market
price will decrease from 4.78 to 4.16; proceeds from landholdings in
the proximity of the market place from 3120 to 640. *With the
reduction of the freight rate the market price and the income from land
drop. With the improvement of transport the level of income from land-
holdings in different locations evens out.* Proceeds from land-holdings
are taken into consideration in these examples only in as far as they
depend on the location of the land. *The extent of the area of supply of
goods is influenced only to a small extent by the rate of freight.*

Although an equal quality of soil for the total area of supply of
goods has been assumed, usage of the land will not be equal in all
locations, but there will be a need, as explained by von Thünen in
The Isolated State, to cultivate such fruit close to the market place
which, due to their great weight or perishability, will incur the
highest transport costs. The total of the market area is therefore
divided into a smaller or larger number of different areas of cultivation which surround the market place concentrically and whose
outermost area will be chosen for animal husbandry whereby the
costs of transport are lowest.

At the outer limit of the area of supply, on the outermost border
of the area of cultivation, proceeds from the land equal zero. At the
inner borderline of this area, at a distance of z'' from the market
place, proceeds of $\gamma f(z' - z'')$ are obtained when γ is the harvest per
unit and f the rate of freight. If at this point the cultivation of
another type of produce begins of which a larger harvest of γ'' is
obtained per unit, then an equal quantity of income must be
obtained from equal proceeds from land holdings. At the inner
border of this second area of cultivation, which is at a distance of z'''
from the market place, savings are made compared to the outer
borderline in freight of $\gamma''f(z'' - z''')$ on the way to the market place

Figure 14

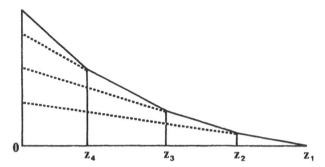

through which the proceeds from land are increased by the following amount:

$$\{\gamma'(z' - z'') + \gamma''(z'' - z''')\}f.$$

With m areas of cultivation, proceeds from land in immediate proximity to the market place is therefore:

$$\{\gamma'(z' - z'') + \gamma''(z'' - z''') + \ldots + \gamma_m z_m\}\, f.$$

The ordinates in Figure 14 represent the level of income from land-holdings across the entire market area.

It suffices to limit examination to two ring-shaped areas of cultivation, an outer one and an inner one. If in the inner area produce is cultivated with utility function $\beta y - \beta_1 y^2$, which is obtained by n' consumers at a priceworthiness w and produced at a cost of p'; then for the determination of the size of the area of cultivation the following two equations are obtained:

$$z'^2 - z''^2 = nw(\alpha/w - p_0 - fz')/\alpha_1\gamma'\pi$$

$$z''^2 = n'w' \{\beta/w' - p' - (\gamma'/\gamma'')(z' - z'')f - fz''\}/2\beta_1\gamma''\pi \quad (118)$$

If for the first good, cultivated in the outer ring, the earlier figures $n = 50{,}000$; $w = 0.5$; $\alpha = 10$, $\alpha_1 = 1/100$; $p_0 = 4$; $\gamma = 4000$; $f = 1/50$ are once more applied, and if for the good, cultivated in the inner circle, $n' = 40{,}000$; $w' = 0.45$; $\beta = 9$, $\beta_1 = 1/20$; $p' = 3$; $\gamma'' = 5000$, it follows that:

$$z'^2 - z''^2 = 1592 - 2z'$$

$$z''^2 = 1170 - 1.1\,z' - 0.28z''.$$

This means that $z' = 50.9$ and $z'' = 33.2$. The market price for the outer good is 5.02; for the inner it is:

$$3 + \frac{1000}{5000}(50.9 - 33.2)\frac{1}{50} + \frac{33.2}{50} = 3.947.$$

Proceeds from land-holdings in close proximity of the market place become $5000(3.947 - 3) = 4735$. If the freight rate is reduced from 1/50 to 1/250 then z' rises to 52.2 and z'' to 34.0. *The borders of the individual areas of cultivation experience an insignificant shift outward due to the improvement of transport facilities.*

If for any of the produce grown in the market area a cheaper *import* from outside occurs, then the market price must remain at the level of the import price and the area of supply must shrink in proportion. If for example goods equal to those produced in the inner area of cultivation were imported at a price of 3.7, then:

$$p' + (\gamma'/\gamma'')(z' - z'')f + fz'' = 3.7$$

or, after applying the numerical values, $0.016z' + 0.004z'' = 0.7$ alongside this equation for the goods from the outer area, would be $z'^2 - z''^2 = 1592 - 2z'$, from which $z' = 41$ and $z'' = 11$. Thus the price for the good from the outer area is 4.82. This calculation shows that due to the situation that the produce from the inner area of cultivation suffered a price decrease of 0.247 because of the import, the good from the outer area of cultivation also dropped in price by 0.2. As is easily realized, the following generally important fact can be stated: *If the price of any of the goods cultivated in the market area is depressed by low-priced imports the prices of all produce drops.*

If, however, the produce of the inner area of cultivation could be exported at a price of 4.2, then:

$$p' + (\gamma/\gamma'')(z' - z'')f + fz'' = 4.2.$$

Accordingly, when substituting numerical values the result must be:

$$0.016z' + 0.004z'' = 1.2$$

so that when considering the equation, $z'^2 - z''^2 = 1592 - 2 z'$, the result is $z' = 62.6$ and $z'' = 49.6$ whereby the market price of the goods from the outer area of production amounts to 4.25; compared to a situation where the export of the goods from the inner area of production was impossible, a rise of 0.3. An important fact is easily recognized: *If the price of produce cultivated anywhere in the market area is increased by the possibility of export, then prices for all other produce of the market area rise.*

31. Supplying Neighbouring Consumer Areas

Between neighbouring consumer areas, the borders of supply areas are determined in response to the varying extent of demand in the individual market areas. In this context the supply areas experience, in comparison with the unlimited market area, more or less considerable restrictions which are followed by an increase in prices and in proceeds from land.

To assess the influence which a restriction of the market area has on the price of produce, let us assume market areas of equal economic importance and at equal distances in all directions so that they form the points of a set of equilateral triangles with a side length of a. Every market area then forms a regular hexagon covering an area of $0.866\, a^2$, and the quantity available to supply a market area, Q, is $0.866\,\gamma a^2$, if γ units of the good are harvested per unit of land. The market price p will now reach a level that causes the demand being exactly equal to the quantity of goods obtained from the market area given as invariable. It is not debatable that the balance between neighbouring market areas can only exist with such a pricing arrangement. With reference to earlier calculations, the following result is therefore arrived at:

$$0.866\,\gamma a^2 = nw\,(\alpha/w - p)/2\alpha_1$$

and from this follows the market price:

$$p = (\alpha - 1.738\,\gamma\,\alpha_1\,a^2/n)/w. \tag{119}$$

At the border of the market areas, i.e. at their corner points which are at a distance of 0.58a from the market place, at a freight rate of f, a price of $p - 0.58fa$ would be paid, that is a profit rate, g, of $p - p_0 - 0.58fa$. The profit of the surface unit or the proceeds from the land-holding is therefore $\gamma(p - p_0 - 0.58fa)$ at this least-favour-

166

able situation of the market area, and $\gamma(p - p_0)$ in the immediate vicinity of the market centre.

While maintaining an unrestricted market area, the following values are used as examples: $n = 50,000$, $\gamma = 4000$, $\alpha = 10$, $\alpha_1 = 1/100$, $w = 0.5$, $p_0 = 4$, $f = 1/50$. If, further, $a = 60$, then the result is $p = 10.0$, the proceeds from land are 24,000 and, at the corners of the borders of the market area, 21,200. *Due to the restriction of the supply area through neighbouring consumer areas, the price of produce and the returns from land are considerably increased, compared to those in the unrestricted market area.*

If it is taken into consideration that $\alpha/2\alpha_1 = b$ is the quantity of the produce which results in maximum utility, and further that $0.866\gamma a^2/n = c$ is the quantity of produce per capita, then (119) can be given as a simple formula for the price of produce:

$$p = 2\alpha_1(b-c)/w. \tag{120}$$

The produce per capita and therefore also the price are dependent on the result of the harvest. If the harvest of each of the landowners is a certain multiple of c, say mc, the gross income is thus mcp. As the preparation and establishment costs, B, depend only to a small extent on the outcome of the harvest, the profit of the landowner can be calculated as follows:

$$G = mcp - B = 2\alpha_1 m\,(b-c)\,c/w - B. \tag{121}$$

This becomes a maximum for $c = b/2$. This means that *the landowner achieves the highest profit when the harvest results in half of that amount which maximizes utility.* It has to be kept in mind that the quantity which maximizes utility is of a size which renders every new increase worthless.

In the calculated example, $b = 500$, $c = (0.866)(4000)(60^2)/50,000 = 250$; that is, according to equation (120), $p = (500 - 250)/25 = 10$, so that the most favourable harvest for the landowner is $mpc = 2500m$. If the harvest γ is only half of 4000, meaning $c = 125$, then the price would be 15, the profit by the landowner amounts to $1875m$; if the harvest increases by half, i.e. to $\gamma = 6000$, and with it $c = 375$, then the price is 5 and the profit for the landowner is $1875m$. The medium-sized harvest $\gamma = 4000$, which covers half of the demand to saturation, supplies in this case the highest profit for the landowner; he does equally badly in the case of a better or a lesser harvest. If, however, the population were smaller, perhaps instead of 50,000 only 40,000, then in the situation of a medium harvest of $\gamma = 4000$, the amount $c = 312.5$ would exceed the most favourable level for the landowner; he would do best with a result of $\gamma = 3200$, remaining below the medium-level harvest. If, on the contrary, the population of the market place were 60,000 instead of 50,000 then the landowner would do best with a harvest result of $\gamma = 4800$, exceeding the medium-level harvest.

In general it can therefore not be maintained that the landowner will enjoy the greatest earnings with a medium-level harvest, but *the profit for the landowner increases where the population relative to the fertility of the soil is low, if the harvest remains below the medium-level value, but where the population density relative to the fertility of the soil is great it improves with better harvests.*

It must be remembered that the full implications of the results developed here apply only to such produce which does not store well and cannot be kept for a longer period of time. In the case of non-perishable produce, stores from previous years are added to the new harvest. Estimated harvests of future years also enter into the formation of prices and the consideration, resting on the estimates, of what quantities, at the prevailing market price, are usefully not released.

The more secluded is a market area from world trade, the lower the price must drop before export becomes possible, and the higher the price can rise before further increases can be curbed by way of imports.

In Figure 15 the harvest results are measured on the abscissa, the resulting unit prices are presented as ordinates below the abscissa and the payments received for the harvest as ordinates above the abscissa; p' represents the import price and p'' the export price.

The more backward are transport facilities or the less accessible is a market area from outside, the greater is the difference between import and export prices. As long as the variation in harvests keeps within the limits at which the market price does not drop to the export price but does not rise to the level of the import price, the net profit for the landholder will not be seriously affected; for the consumer, however, very considerable price variations will occur. But as soon as the variation in the harvest exceeds the limits at which import or export are possible, then considerably larger or smaller profits are experienced by the farmer, while the consumer, indepen-

Figure 15

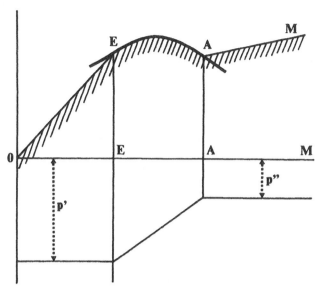

dent of the harvest result, has to pay the almost unchanged import or export price. *The more transport facilities are perfected, i.e. the more the market area is brought under the influence of global exchange regulating prices, the smaller the difference becomes between import and export prices, the greater the movement up and down of the farmer's net profit will become and the steadier the price will be for the consumer.*

If the size of the medium harvest is so small that imports become necessary, or so large that exports become possible, if in Figure 15 therefore it is situated between the lines OE or AM, then the net profit of the farmer depends to a considerable extent on the outcome of the harvest. But if the medium harvest result lies within the line EA so that neither import nor export can occur, then the net profit of agriculture is exposed to mere small changes due to varying harvest results, the more so the bigger the difference between import and export prices is.

Even in a limited market area the division into von Thünen's cultivation areas proceeds in a very similar way to that in an unlimited market area. For the purpose of demonstration it will suffice to suppose two cultivation areas, of which the inner, circular one may have a radius of z. At the borderline where both areas meet, a net profit $\gamma'(p - p_0 - fz)$ will be achieved in the outer area per surface unit. If the same net profit is to be achieved also for the produce cultivated in the inner area of which γ'' units per surface unit are harvested, then an amount γ'/γ'' $(p - p_0 - fz)$ must be added to the production costs of p'. Maintaining the expressions adopted in Chapter 30 for the determination of z and p, the following equations are arrived at:

$$\gamma'' \pi z^2 = n'w'\{\beta/w' - p' - (\gamma'/\gamma'')(p - p_0 - fz) - fz\}/2\beta_1$$

$$\gamma'\,(0.866\,a^2 - \pi z^2) = nw\,(\alpha/w - p)/z\alpha_1 \qquad (122)$$

and after substituting the earlier values:

$$z^2 = 1390 - 55\,p - 0.28z$$

$$994 - z^2 = 1270 - 63.6p$$

from which $p = 12.6$ and $z = 16$. The market price of the interior good is $p' + (\gamma'/\gamma'')\,(p - p_0 - fz) + fz$, that is, 9.94.

The limits of the areas of cultivation are influenced to an almost unnoticeable degree by the freight rate, so are the market prices, but in contrast, the proceeds from land-holdings are increased due to improvements in the local transport facilities and to a higher degree in proportion to increasing distance from the market place. At the farthest distance from the market place $= (0.58)(60) = 34.8$ at a freight rate $f = 1/50$, $p_0 = 4$, $p = 12.6$ and $\gamma' = 4000$, the proceeds from land-holdings $= 4000\,(12.6 - 4 - 34.8/50) = 31,632$ but increases due to lowering the freight rate to $1/250$, resulting in 33,843.

As proved in Chapter 30, prices of all other produce as well as the borders of the various cultivation areas change, as soon as the produce of any given cultivation area is imported or exported. The increase of duty on cereal crops must for example cause a price increase for all produce and, with a growth in the cultivation of cereals, cause amongst other things a reduction in livestock breeding. Nothing is therefore more rash and erroneous than drawing the conclusion 'often made' that a reduction in the cattle-breeding industry of a country reflects a threatening situation for agriculture as a whole.

The size of individual market areas depends on the distance of the market places from one another, on the size of the population and its affluence. A well-populated and affluent market extends its area at the cost of its neighbouring markets of lesser economic importance. This extension can only occur by way of increased prices and through it, increased proceeds from land. The neighbouring smaller markets, whose area is reduced in the direction of the larger market, extend in the opposite direction, in order to replace lost ground, which can only happen through a corresponding increase in prices. *The increase of market prices in a major city is followed by increases in neighbouring smaller markets and from these down again, but to a rather rapidly decreasing extent, to further-distant places.* The level of earnings from the land is essentially dependent on the ratio between density and distribution of population on the one hand and the fertility of the land on the other.

32. Freight Rates

In the transport of goods by road and waterways, which are access-ible for anyone's use, the freight rate will be reduced by competition to a level at which the weakest of the businesses will no longer achieve any profit. With rail transport, such an arrangement for freight rates is ruled out because each railway line is operated by one business only. However, with the current expansion of the rail network it is possible to use, for longer distances, different routes, and competition will soon give way to agreements between the few owners, even if the lines to be chosen from belong to different owners. The owners who could be led to compete will be enabled, through such agreements, to secure the monopoly for their busi-nesses. In that case the freight rate can be fixed in accordance with the basic rule for business profit developed in Chapter 22.

If the price of a good at its place of origin is p, at a freight rate of f, at a distance z from the place of origin, the demand developing at this distance is some function of this price for which, in accordance with earlier suppositions, may be written:

$$x = \gamma(\alpha/w - p - fz).$$

The difference between the maximum price α/w at which the first unit of goods finds buyers, and the price p to be paid at the place of origin, was (in Chapter 27) called dispatch value and denoted v.

If the dispatch of goods were taken on by the manufacturer at costs of f_0 per ton kilometre, then the furthest distance of dispatch would be $z_0 - v/f_0$. With an increase in the freight rate above the manufacturing costs, the furthest dispatch distance is reduced to $z' = v/f$. With a rise in the manufacturing surplus per transport unit $f - f_0$, the number of dispatched units drops because not only the furthest dispatch distance becomes shorter, but due to a higher price demand also drops. There exists therefore a certain freight rate by which the highest manufacturing surplus is achieved. But in the determination of this several different cases must be distinguished.

172

To begin with, a case will be considered where the sales area of goods is not limited in any way by competition with other goods which are sent in from foreign places. The number of transport units (ton kilometres) to be covered to achieve supply within the sales area with a radius of z' is therefore:

$$V = 2\,\gamma\pi \int_0^{z'} (v - fz)\, z^2\, dz$$
$$= 2\,\gamma\pi\, (vz'^3/3 - fz'^4/4)$$

or, as $z' = v/f$:

$$V = \gamma\pi v^4/6f^3 \tag{123}$$

and therefore the manufacturing surplus which is achieved by dispatch of these goods is:

$$U = \gamma\pi v^4(f - f_0)/6f^3. \tag{124}$$

This becomes a maximum with $f = 1.5f_0$, at which

$$U' = 2\gamma\pi v^4/81f_0^2. \tag{125}$$

This formula, which is as simple as it is important, says: *For goods with a sales area limited only by freight rates, the most favourable freight rate is equal to 1.5 times the amount of running costs.* The running costs here are to be determined excluding the interest on the investment capital as far as this is independent of the extent of the traffic.

This formula is all the more important as the condition on which it is based applies to a large extent to railway transport, and also especially because its correctness is independent of the form taken by the equation for demand. The same formula $f = 1.5\, f_0$ is also arrived at with the supposition that the demand is independent of the goods price, anywhere equalling γ, because then the number of transport units is:

$$V = 2\,\gamma\pi \int_0^{z'} z^2 dz$$
$$= 2\,\gamma\pi v^3/3f^3$$

so that

Figure 16

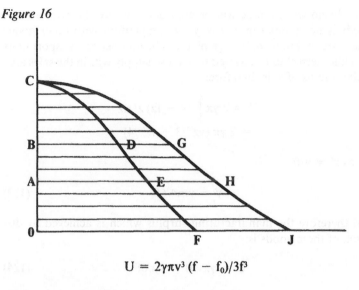

$$U = 2\gamma\pi v^3 (f - f_0)/3f^3$$

which reaches its maximum for $f = 1.5\,f_0$.

But it is imaginable that goods of variable 'sales density', which is decreasing due to some increase in price, can be replaced by a large number of different goods of which each has a constant 'sales density' but different dispatch values. In Figure 16 in which the abscissae indicate the dispatch distances, at a freight rate f, the level of the 'sales density' may be taken to be demonstrated in the form of the ordinates of the curve CDEF for any other, smaller freight rate, through the ordinates of curve CGHJ, then one variety of goods with a sales density at the place of origin $\gamma = CO$ can be imagined to be replaced by goods n, each of which has a sales density of γ/n at the place of origin retaining it unchanged up to the furthest dispatch distance. The furthest dispatch distances of each of these different goods are then measured in the direction of the abscissa up to the curves.

From equation (125) it can be seen that: *The level of the highest manufacturing profit is achieved at the most favourable rate of freight, growing by the fourth power of the dispatch value of the goods.* This explains the great importance of goods of high dispatch value and great sales density, as for example coal for the running of the railway system. For a rail business the calculated freight rate of $f = 1.5\,f_0$ will only be most favourable if the borders of its rail network are not exceeded by the furthest dispatch distance. If the railway of an owner did not extend to the furthest dispatch distance of z' but only to a distance of z'' all round, then his business profit would be:

$$U = 2\,\gamma\pi\,(f - f_0)\left(\int_0^{z''} z^2\,dz + z''\int_{z''}^{z'} z\,dz\right)$$

$$= \gamma\pi\,(f - f_0)z''(z'^2 - z''^2/3)$$

or, because $z' = v/f$:

$$U = \gamma\pi\,(f - f_0)\,z''\,(v^2/f^2 - z''2/3). \tag{126}$$

This becomes a maximum for:

$$f^3 + 3\,(v/z'')^2\,f - 6\,(v/z')^2\,f_0 = 0.$$

As the furthest dispatch distance is $z' = v/f$, it follows that:

$$6f_0/\{3 + (z''/z')^2\}. \tag{127}$$

Depending on the extent of the railnet, the most favourable rate of freight will lie between $f = 2f_0$ and $f = 1.5\,f_0$. From this the quite remarkable fact follows that *large railway companies can set, to their own advantage, lower freight rates than smaller railway companies.*

This fact becomes even more accentuated for *branch lines.* Let us suppose the simplest case, that the branch line has only one station so that all goods travel the full length z'' of the line. Then, at a freight rate of f' charged by the branch line, when arriving at the main line an amount of $v - f'z''$ of the dispatch value v of the goods is available for further dispatch on the main line so that the quantity of goods transferring to the main line is:

$$Q = 2\,\gamma\pi\int_0^{z'} (v - f'z'' - fz)\,z\,dz$$

$$= \gamma\pi\,(v - f'z'')\,z'^2 - fz'^3/3)$$

or, because $z' = (v - f'z'')/f$:

$$Q = \gamma\pi\,(v - f'z'')^3/3f^2.$$

The running profit of the branch line is therefore:

$$U = z''(f' - f_0)$$
$$= \gamma\pi z'' \, (f' - f_0)(v - f'z'')^3/3f^2 \qquad (128)$$

which becomes a maximum for:

$$f' = 3f_0/4 + v/4z''.$$

As $v = z_0 f_0$, it follows that:

$$f = (3/4 + z_0/4z'')f_0. \qquad (129)$$

For instance, if a branch line with a length of $z'' = 1/10 \, z_0$, $f' = 3.25 \, f_0$ and for $z'' = 1/20 \, z_0$ at $f' = 5.74 \, f_0$.

If the branch line does not operate independently, but together with the main line, it would be to the advantage of the company to draw a lot of traffic across from the branch line to the main line. The incoming quantity of traffic to the main line (in ton kilometres) is:

$$V = 2\gamma\pi \int_0^{z'} (v - f'z'' - fz) \, z^2 dz$$
$$= \gamma\pi(v - f'z'')^4/6f^3.$$

The profit derived from the traffic directed from the branch line the main line is:

$$U = \gamma\pi z''(f' - f_0)(v - f'z'')^3/3f^2 + \gamma\pi(f - f_0)(v - f'z'')^4/6f^3. \qquad (130)$$

This becomes a maximum for

$$f' = (3z''f_0 f + zvf_0 - vf)/2z''(f + f_0)$$

and if the freight rate charged on the main line is $f = 1.5f_0$ it becomes:

$$f' = (9 + z_0/z'')/10f_0 \qquad (131)$$

for example for $z'' = 1/10 \, z_0$ the result is $f' = 1.9 \, f_0$, for $z'' = 1/20 \, z_0$ it is $f' = 2.9 \, f_0$.

The freight rates for a branch line which is operated on account of the mainline railway must be set at a lower rate than if the owner operates the branch line on his own separate account. The most favourable freight rates for branch lines will, even in the first case, amount to higher rates than those for the main line.

For short branch lines the introduction of the most favourable freight rates could not be implemented in consideration of competition from road transport. If the sales area of certain goods cannot be infinitely extended through lowering of freight rates, but if instead it is limited by foreign goods from another source of supply, then the most favourable freight rate is higher than 1.5 f_0. If in consideration of competition from goods entering from foreign sources the sales area can be extended to a radius of only z″ then the business profit is:

$$U = (f - f_0) \int_0^{z^{\prime\prime}} 2\gamma\pi(v - fz) z^2 dz$$
$$= 2\gamma\pi (f - f_0)(v/3 - f2^{\prime\prime}/4)z^{\prime\prime 3}. \qquad (132)$$

This becomes a maximum for:

$$f = f_0/2 + 2v/3z^{\prime\prime}$$
$$= (0.5 + 2z_0/3z^{\prime\prime})f_0. \qquad (133)$$

For example, for z″ = 1/6 z_0 to f = 4.5 f_0. For the borderline case z″ = 2/3z_0 the restriction due to competition from foreign goods ceases and becomes f = 1.5 f_0.

Finally, consider the case of supply of a market town. As the reduction in freight rates can expand the market territory insignificantly, so that the quantity of goods to be transported will be only marginally increased, the railway administration will not profit by reducing the freight rate to a level lower than is necessary to prevent further use of roads and existing waterways.

The earlier calculations demonstrate that generally the most favourable rate of freight on railways is 1.5 times the amount of running costs, but that in order to achieve the highest operating profit the freight rate for some means of transport has to be set at a higher freight rate.

When charging the freight rate f = 1.5 f_0 only two-thirds of the furthest dispatch distance z_0 is used which can be reached when only the operating costs are covered. It is now worth considering the extension of the rail net to destinations at distances beyond $2z_0/37$

for which, when maintaining the freight rate $f = 3f_0/2$ transport is impossible, and to settle instead for these long distances for a lower rate of profit. This thought leads to so-called *differential tariffs* which reduce the freight rate at a ratio to the distance unit.

If the variable rate of freight is set at $f' - f'z$, freight at a distance z is $fz - fz^2$, then the operating profit for the entire sales area is:

$$U = 2\gamma\pi \int_0^z (v - f^2 + f'z^2)(f - f^2 - f_0)z^2 dz. \tag{134}$$

Sales become zero when $f_0 z' - fz' + f'z'^2 = 0$, so that it must be:

$$f' = (f - f_0)/z'.$$

If this value of f' is introduced after integration and it is investigated at which value of f the operating profit becomes a maximum, it will be found that $f = 2f_0$, i.e. $f' = f_0/z' = f_0^2/v$. In general the freight rate for a rational differential tariff must therefore be:

$$f'' = (2 - f_0 z/v)f_0 \tag{135}$$

whereby an operating profit is achieved of:

$$U' = \gamma\pi v^4/30 f_2^0. \tag{136}$$

As comparison with (125) demonstrates, this will come to 1.35 times that which can be achieved at a most favourable invariable freight rate $f = 1.5 f_0$. The introduction of such a freight rate steadily reducing with increasing distance is, however, made difficult because the dispatch value of the goods must be known in order to calculate the correct proportion by which the freight rate must be reduced with increasing distance.

In all investigations into the most favourable freight rate it has so far been assumed that the costs for departing and arriving goods were charged together with a per kilometre rate in the form of a *clearance charge* (dispatch charges). It remains now to find out whether it may not be more useful to level the clearance charges not at the same rate as the costs for incoming and outgoing goods, but to set them at a different rate, be it lower or higher.

If the costs arising from the incoming and outgoing of goods are A_0 per unit and if the clearance charges amount to A, then for the distance z a freight $A + fz$ is countered by operating costs of $A_0 + f_0z$ and at this dispatch distance an operating profit $A - A_0 + fz - f_0z$ is achieved. The quantity of goods dependent on the rate of freight is $\gamma(\alpha/w - p - A - fz)$. By introducing the dispatch value v in the calculation of which the manufacturing price p of the goods was seen to be inclusive of the amount for the incoming and outgoing A_0 so that $v = \alpha/w - p - A_0$ is assumed, the quantity of goods $\gamma(v + A_0 - A - fz)$ results, thus achieving an operating profit at the distance z of:

$$u = \gamma(v + A_0 - A - fz)(A - A_0 + fz - f_0z). \qquad (137)$$

If we differentiate with respect to A and f we obtain, after setting to zero both differential quotients, two equations from which the most favourable values for the clearance charges and the freight rate per kilometre derive:

$$A = A_0 + v/2 \qquad (138)$$

$$f = f_0/2. \qquad (139)$$

Therefore the highest achievable operating profit is:

$$u = \gamma(v - f_0z)^2/4 \qquad (140)$$

and for the entire sales area is:

$$U = 0.5\gamma\pi \int_0^{z'} (v - f_0z)^2 z\,dz.$$

Substituting $z' = v/f_0$ this becomes:

$$U = \gamma\pi v^4/24f_0^2. \qquad (141)$$

That means: *The highest operating profit is achieved when the freight rate per kilometre is set at only half of the operating costs per kilometre, but a clearance charge is made which exceeds the costs for incoming and outgoing of the goods by half the dispatch value of the goods.* The operating profit will then equal one and eleven-sixteenths compared to the setting of the freight rate in which the clearance charge is levelled at the amount of costs arising from incoming and outgoing of goods and the freight rate per kilometre at the then most favourable level of $f = 1.5\,f''$ and amounts, compared to the differential tariff, to 1.25 times.

The fact that the freight rate for shorter distances is higher than the rates for transport on long-distance highways speaks against the introduction of such a way of freight pricing. Investigation teaches however that *to achieve a high operating profit the clearance charge must not be set too low and the freight rate per kilometre must be kept as low as possible.*

The freight rate most favourable to the railway company is naturally not at the same time the most favourable from the aggregate economic point of view. To find the *economically most favourable rate of freight* it has first of all to be observed that at a freight cost of fz demand and therefore also the quantity of goods dispatched over a distance z is:

$$x = \gamma(\alpha/w - p - fz). \tag{142}$$

At a given distance z demand commences when the rate of freight is reduced to $f' = (\alpha/w - p)/z$, whereby the price paid for the goods is $p + f'z = \alpha/w$.

If the freight rate is assumed to be variable, the quantity of goods being dispatched at a reduction of the freight rate by df, will increase as can be deduced from (142), by:

$$dx = \gamma z df. \tag{143}$$

As the price $p + fz$ is paid per unit of goods, it follows that a price of $(p + fz)dx = (p + fz)\gamma z df$ is offered for the increase in the quantity of goods.

If suddenly the freight rate is reduced from f to f'' the goods price will change from $p + fz$ to $p + fz''$ – this means that the consumer of the goods makes a saving on each unit of $(f - f'')$, therefore on a quantity of goods dx the amount: $(f - f'')\,zdx$ or after taking (143) into consideration:

$$(f - f'')\gamma z^2 df.$$

From the freight rate $f' = (\alpha/w - p)/z = v/z$, for which the dispatch of goods commences to a destination at a distance of z, from charging the freight rate f'', the savings on the price of goods which benefits the consumer, is:

$$e = \gamma z^2 \int_{f''}^{f} (f - f'')df$$

$$= 0.5\gamma z^2(f - f'')^2.$$

If $zf' = \alpha/w - p$ is introduced, it follows that:

$$e = 0.5\gamma(\alpha/w - p - f''z)^2.$$

As $\gamma(\alpha/w - p - f''z)$ is the quantity of goods at the freight rate of f'' to a destination at a distance of z therefore the amount of:

$$0.5 (\alpha/w - p - f''z)$$

is gained for the consumer of the goods for every transported unit, that is half the difference between the price α/w, at which the demand for the goods commences, and the price $p + f''z$ which must in reality be paid. If, as earlier, $\alpha/w - p = v$ is introduced, then it follows that:

$$e = 0.5\gamma(v - f''z)^2.$$

In this way, we arrive at the benefit for consumers in the entire sales area at a freight rate of f'':

$$E = \gamma\pi \int_0^{z'} (v - f''z)^2 z dz$$

as $z' = v/f''$ the result is:

$$E = \gamma\pi v^4/12f''^2. \tag{144}$$

The running profit achieved at a freight rate of f'' is:

$$U = \gamma\pi v^4 (f'' - f_0)/6f''^3$$

and therefore the total economic gain is:

$$G = E + U = \gamma\pi v^4 (3/f''^2 - 2f_0/f''^3)/12. \tag{145}$$

A maximum is reached, when $f'' = f_0$, of:

$$G' = \gamma\pi v^4/12f_0^2. \tag{146}$$

From an economic point of view it is therefore most profitable when freight costs are raised only to the level of the operating costs. This formula applies as well to any other form of the demand equation.

When the freight rate per kilometre $= 1.5\, f_0$ is charged which is most favourable to the railway company, the total economic gain comes to $5\gamma\pi\, v^4/81f_0^2$, i.e. it forms only 20/27 of the amount which is obtainable. *This fact demonstrates most convincingly that railways are a service which should never be left to private enterprise.*

Certainly, even for the state as owner of the railways, it is not to be recommended to go as low as the operating-cost level in the establishment of the freight rates to achieve the greatest general economic usefulness. If this method were adopted, interest on the investment capital would have to be raised through additional taxation which would be perceived by the population as far more oppressive than raising this interest through higher freight rates. But the state can approach a level of the economically most favourable freight rate to such a degree as seems acceptable with consideration of the taxation policies.

A quantity of goods $\gamma(v - (2 - f_0z/v)f_0z) = \gamma(v - f_0z)^2/v$ is transported to a distance z at the differential tariff so favourable to the railway management. Consumers gain for each unit $0.5\,(v - 2f_0z + f_0^2z^2/v) = (v - f_0z)^2/2v$ the railway management gains $(2 - f_0z/v)f_0z - f_0z = (v - f_0z)f_0z/v$, i.e. consumers and railway management together gain $(v - f_0z)(v + f_0z)/2v$ per unit. For the entire sales area the economic gain is therefore:

$$G = (\gamma\pi/v^2) \int_0^{z'} (v - f_02)^3 (v + f_0z)z\,dz.$$

Substituting $z' = v/f_0$, this becomes:

$$G = \gamma\pi v^4/15f_0^2. \tag{147}$$

As the economic gain at an invariable freight rate per kilometre of $f = 1.5\, f_0$ amounts to only $5\gamma\pi v^4/81f_0^2$ it means that *the differential tariff so favourable to the railway management is preferable as well from a total economic point of view.*

33. Effects of Improved Transport Facilities

The often-discussed effects of the improvement of transport facilities are probably assessed in the most detailed manner in *Railways and Their Effects* by Karl Knies published in 1853, and more recently by Emil Sax in *The Means of Transport*. These effects, which are reflected in the most profound and decisive manner in the development of economic life as well as in the formation of social conditions, in fact in the entire cultural development of humankind, are of such a multifarious nature that it is difficult to demonstrate them in one total, all-inclusive depiction. The present task is limited to stressing those most important effects which often in their different directions coincided in their emphasis, but often negated one another or at least impaired their results. In spite of the variety of appearances which are caused by the perfection of the means of transport, all of them can be reduced to the same simple rule, that is to the *reduction of the importance of distance*. The command over distance is extended and thereby every expression of activity, which found its limits of development in spatial obstacles, can be extended and furthered. In contrast the effort of every process which depends on spatial isolation is reduced and weakened.

As an immediate result of the improvement of means of transport there evolves *an increase in pleasure due to a reduction in the effort necessary to obtain goods*. This situation must necessarily counter any increases in the price of goods due to other causes. Of even more decisive influence on the wellbeing of humankind is the reduction in the variation of prices. The limits between which a price must remain for a given geographic position are determined by the import and export prices, the difference between one and the other is reduced by a lowering of the freight rate. But the smaller the difference between the import and the export prices becomes, the more must the number of varieties of produce grow which in spite of varying harvests can be exported on a continuous basis or are exposed to

183

imports so that their prices move no longer between the extremes of import and export prices, but depend entirely on the movements of the export price or are subjected only to the fluctuations in import prices. *The ease of meeting an imbalance due to local harvest failures and plentiful supplies elsewhere due to bumper crops releases human-kind from the dreadful threat of famine* which, because of under-developed transport facilities, still depopulates whole provinces in China and India.

The beneficial reduction in time-related price fluctuations causes, however, the income of the farmer to vary more extremely and to be more dependent on the result of harvests. His average annual income suffers through improvements of transport facilities only when cultivating produce which is exposed to competition from imports, where produce cannot be grown in sufficient quantity in the local soil or produced at a low enough price. As much as every improvement of transport, which makes access from outside easier, must be damaging, so in contrast the cultivation of produce which can be exported, due to improved means of transport which facili-tate access to foreign markets, will prove to be more rewarding. The continuing improvements of transport will therefore force the land-owner to turn more and more towards the cultivation of produce which is suitable for export, and discontinue any form of cultivation which has to compete with imported goods. An exception to this general rule occurs only in cases where import is due only to the fact that the local soil is too poor to satisfy demand, as applies for example in viniculture in Germany; or if export takes place only because production exceeds local demand. More precisely it should therefore be expressed as follows: *Due to the improvement of trans-port facilities, agriculture must turn more and more towards the pro-duction of produce for which soil conditions and climate offer the most favourable conditions*, and must abandon the cultivation of fruit for which local conditions are less favourable. While all needs had to be satisfied by local sources, as far as climate and local soils permitted, when the means of transport were underdeveloped, the characteris-tic of any soil will now be allowed to reach full potential because of the perfection of the means of transport. A *local division of labour* must develop with ever-increasing clarity for cultivation of the land. But this effect must manifest itself to an even higher degree for all areas of manufacturing.

The production of goods taking place under favourable conditions extends its sales area, due to the improvement of transport, at the expense of neighbouring centres of production which are based on less-favourable foundations. The producer in less-favourable circumstances can only continue to exist as long as he enjoys the effective protection of poor roads; he is easily defeated as soon as he comes, due to improved transport facilities, within the reach of the stronger competitor, just as a fortress loses all meaning as soon as the attacking guns have found a range which allows bombardment from the neighbouring hills.

The extension of the sales area for the goods manufactured under favourable conditions, due to improved transport facilities, increases profit and, following this, the incentive for new manufacturers to establish themselves in the same location thus entering into competition. With growing numbers of manufacturers the profit margin must be reduced, which leads to a further extension of the sales area, to a further forcing back of competition from foreign sources.

In this way, centres of manufacture form which specialize in specific branches of manufacture and which offer the most favourable conditions for the respective firm. This *local grouping of branches of manufacture* provides such important advantages for the perfection of manufacturing processes, for the formation of a well-trained nucleus of workers, for commercial trading etc. that, once initiated by the improvement of transport facilities, it will develop in an ever-more-pronounced manner. Though it, *the division of labour* will be promoted. The division of manufacture into a series of independent plants will take place, supporting one another in a step-by-step structure; in place of a woollen mill which handles the product from the washing of wool to the dispatch of the finished products, there will be specialized wool-washing plants, combining works, spinning mills, dyeing plants and weaving mills. In the immediate vicinity of a distinct branch of manufacture, auxiliary industry will settle, so that the entire economic character of an area will follow the dominant branch of manufacture.

The perfection of transport is therefore followed by a stronger shaping of a local character both for manufacture and agriculture. As a result of an extended market, the exploitation of mineral deposits, hitherto able to be dispatched only short distances because of their heavy weight, reaches a quite extraordinary volume. Some of these mineral deposits which now contribute regularly to the increase in nations' wealth have been discovered for exploitation only because of the perfection of the means of transport.

Like the companies engaged in the extraction of mineral deposits, so locally grouped branches of manufacture take on the character of large concerns. The old traditions in cottage industry become untenable, the shackles of guild systems are broken, the workshops enlarge into factories. The order of labour, firmly structured in the guilds of crafts, even if relying on a restricted base, dissolved and, with this, the strictly ordered division of human society, without new, satisfactory forms having been found. Such a mighty re-formation reaching into all economic and social conditions cannot take place in one bold stroke, not without long continuing struggles. Unavoidable are, on the one hand, demands beyond a reasonable goal, and on the other hand, an exaggerated holding-on to established ways. But the troubles and dangers of the struggle must not lead to overestimation of the cosy peace of 'the good old days', they must not dim the realization of the great economic and cultural advances which have been made in the train of the *development of the large concern*. The progress which in all its repercussions can hardly be sufficiently acknowledged, which alone was made through the introduction of the large concern, consists of the replacement of human labour by mechanical labour powered by nature. Humankind is thereby, if not completely, so essentially released from the burden of agonizing physical labour under which it sighed for millenia. Many useful goods are accessible for general use because of cheap mechanical labour which, due to their high prices, used to be obtained only by a privileged few. *The enjoyment of life is increased not only by the release from physial labour but also by the availability of new consumer goods for wide sections of human society.*

Victory in the intensified competitive struggle of production of goods can only be won through the improvement of manufacturing processes by which an improvement in the quality and a cheaper method of production of goods can be attained. The many-faceted and continuing efforts of the intellectual input leading to this goal can succeed in proportion to the extent of the endeavour only in a large concern. Nevertheless, the large concern cannot be considered beneficial in every respect. The relentless fight against small enterprise as well as against competing large concerns has destroyed the property of many individuals and often impairs the nation's wealth severely. *It is one of the important tasks of economic policies to abandon in this respect, too, the 'laissez faire' attitude* and, as far as possible, to intervene in a protective and monitoring role. The perfection of manufacturing processes gained for the large concern, then, benefits those branches of manufacture which, in accord with their nature, can only ever be conducted in small enterprises, be it that their products perish too quickly or that they have to be designed to specifications with individually varying demands, or that artistic ability is needed for their manufacture. It must also be kept in mind that in order to achieve the lowest production price, there is a limit to the change from a small enterprise into a large concern for every kind of production of goods, which must not, as was proved at the end of Chapter 29, be overstepped.

Through the improvement of transport facilities, agricultural enterprise must, just as is the case of manufacturing enterprise, also change more and more to large enterprise, if not to the same compelling degree. Agricultural enterprise can maintain its presence in the face of imports only through the utmost reduction in operating costs, which necessitates the introduction of mechanization which can be implemented to a sufficient level only in large enterprises. As mentioned earlier, it must be remembered that the price of produce in a situation of fully developed transport facilities is regulated by the world market and operates within narrow limits so that the net profit in agriculture depends greatly on the outcome of each harvest. This variation in annual income can be borne only by the large landholders equipped with sufficient capital, while the small landowner easily falls victim to the profiteer and is destroyed. Here, too, as in manufacture, a healthy economic policy executed with clarity and energy must apply to all means to secure the clear advantages of the large enterprise without allowing its devastating consequences to develop for social order and human welfare.

Agriculture is threatened by another danger emanating from a restructuring of *settlement conditions* due to the improvement of transport facilities. At the time of underdeveloped means of transport the populations of cities suffered considerably under the severe fluctuations of food prices due to the outcome of local harvests, while the population in the countryside was exposed to only relatively small fluctuations in their income because prices rose severely at times of poor harvests, just as they fell at times of good harvests. In order to protect themselves against this deplorable state of affairs as far as possible, towns and cities were forced to engage in agriculture and animal husbandry, which resulted in keeping their growth within reasonable bounds. The limitations of the sales area for their products also hindered a stronger growth of towns. With the concentration of large masses of population in towns and cities the turnover of manufactured goods was extraordinarily facilitated which had to lead to ever-increasing manufacturing activities and an increasing growth of towns and cities. Towns could previously spread and flourish only where, due to waterways, good natural transport facilities existed.

As a result of the perfection of the means of transport, conditions in cities and in the countryside reversed completely. The prices for produce, now no longer dependent on the quality of local harvests but kept at an even level on the world market, secure a more regular standard of living for the population of cities, while the wellbeing of the population in the countryside depends on the changeable results of harvests. Mass migration of the country population to cities, where the new labour force was welcomed due to the increase in manufacturing activity, was the result of this situation. The ensuing drop in population in the countryside, aggravated by overseas emigration, heightens the urgency for the introduction of farm machinery and hastens the disappearance of the small land-holder. The growth of cities and towns leads undisputably to a faster rate of development of civilization, causes the implementation of the most elaborate facilities for the furthering of health, comfort and pleasure, effects in the liveliest way the furthering of all manner of the arts and sciences. But the intensity of the fight for survival, increasing with the greater density of population, the unrest stemming from the haste to acquire and the addiction to pleasure, leading to overstimulation, vice and crime, are certainly not to be counted amongst the beneficial results of the perfection of the means of transport. But even this phenomenon is not discouraging because evil has lost the protection of seclusion and isolation.

Even if the detachment of man from local concerns has now reached a level in civilized countries where the ideas of 'home' and 'homeland' carry hardly any meaning for his emotional life, for civilization and economic condition, so, nevertheless, the ease with which man can move from one locality to another has given him a heightened control over nature, has led him to live a considerably enhanced lifestyle. All the beauty of nature, the treasures of knowledge and the arts, which were previously accessible to a privileged few only, are becoming more and more the common property of all humankind. The seeds of thoughts and ideas which previously would have been buried where they were born remain in circulation until they fall on fertile soil for their development.

Index